Wild Amazon

A photographer's incredible journey

As written, photographed, experienced and **lived** by

Nick Gordon

Wild Amazon

Publishers
Evans Mitchell Books
The Old Forge
16 Church Street
Rickmansworth, Herts
WD3 1DH United Kingdom
info@senateconsulting.co.uk
www.embooks.co.uk

© Evans Mitchell Books. Printed 2007

Text & Photographs
© Nick Gordon 2004

Editor
Sarah Hoggett

Design
Darren Westlake at **TU ink** www.tuink.co.uk

Origination, Printing and Binding
KWF Printing Pte Ltd, Singapore

ISBN 1 901268 30 6   9 781901 268300

This book is dedicated to Anglia Television's
natural history film unit, especially to the
devoted people who helped me survive my
years in Amazonia.

Survival 1961–2001: Lord Buxton, Lady Buxton,
Colin Willock, David McCall, Mike Hay, Jeremy
Bradshaw, Graham Creelman, Caroline Brett, Mike
Linley, Malcolm Penny, Petra Regent, Alan Bray,
Margaret Bray, Michael Holmes, Ray Holmes, John
Farr, Carl Hall, Tom Walshe, Mervyn Warner, Peter
Schofield, Vivica Parsons, Fay Armstrong, Anne
Bagenall, Phoebe Cameron, Frank Cross, Sue Davis,
Pat Finney, Kerry Flynn, Angela Rule, Kathryn Shreeve,
Alison Aitken, Mark Anderson, Roy Handford,
Howard Marshall, Les Parry, Carol O'Callaghan, Rob
Harrington, Ken Hansford, Lawrence Terroni, Ramon
Burrows, Franklyn Dale, Eric Howard, Libby Snow,
John Thurley, Rod McCann, Oonah Newbury, Paul
Willock, George Hobbs, Crispin Sadler, Pat Sands,
Sinjee St. John, Biddy Wood, David Haynes, Olwen
Gillespie, Andy Bee, Simon Boardman, Caroline
Butler, Colin Chandler, Sue Harrison, Gill Conway,
Caroline Dunne, Martin Banks, Saskia Webster, Isobel
Weller-Poley, Liz Thomson, Frances Whitby, Annie
Price, Terry Groom, Karin Robertson, Ruth Dodds, Ann
Williams, Eve Horan, Sue Kelly, Vic Hawkins, Richard
Osborne, Pauline Miller, Barbara Masters, Judith
Hellary, Kelvin Page, Anthea Olsen, Jacinth O'Donnell,
Roy Hunt, Sarah Lazarus, Sue Ingle, Joanna Mintey,
Abi Hopkinson, Ann Starling, Ross Thornycroft, Emma
Ross, Tim Peel, James Peters, Alison Hale, Mark Golly,
Allison Garrity, Paula Frances, Allison Bean, Shane
Allen, Willie Johnson, Veronica Birley, Stanley Joseph,
John Gooders, Caroline Weaver, Colin Chapman,
Philip Black, Mary Plage and the *Survival* USA team.

Contents

TRI

With kind permiss
the *Daily Tel*

Nick Gordon

Wildlife film-maker who fell in love with the rainforest and spent seven years studying the life of the jaguar

Daily Telegraph
Obituaries, 4 May 2004

Nick Gordon, who died on 25 April 2004, was one of Britain's most successful natural history film-makers; his particular passion was the Brazilian Amazon, where he spent seven years working on a documentary about the life of the jaguar.

His chosen way of life was uncomfortable and dangerous. He endured frequent bouts of malaria, as well as dengue fever and hepatitis; he was bitten by an alligator and by snakes; in Sierra Leone he was shot at when he found himself caught in the middle of a civil war.

Although Gordon had strong views about man's depredations of the planet, saying that he was driven by an "eco-message", he nevertheless denied that his prime purpose was missionary: "I don't preach... I entertain."

While his chief interest was always in the animal kingdom, Gordon also became fascinated by the indigenous peoples whom he encountered. In 1991 he came across the Piaroa people in Venezuela, who worship and eat the goliath tarantula, the world's largest spider.

He and his assistant, Gordon Buchanan, participated in a feast of roasted tarantula in the Piaroas' funeral cave, surrounded by the mummified corpses of the Indians' ancestors. Gordon, who was making his film *Tarantula!* at the time, reported that this delicacy tasted "a bit like crab", while the abdomen was "rather like a poached egg".

Nicholas Cranber Gordon was born at Twickenham on May 9 1952. When he was nine the family moved to Blackpool, where his parents ran a restaurant, and he was sent to school at Lindisfarne College, north Wales. His first notion was to train as a chartered surveyor; but at the age of 19 he joined a sub-aqua club, which inspired him to seek a career as a wildlife cameraman. He recalled: "From the moment I put my head under the water and saw this extraordinary new world, I was seized with the desire to capture these wonderful images."

While he began making amateur wildlife films, he and his first wife, Ann, ran a fish and chip shop in Blackpool. When he was 26 he landed a job as a news cameraman for the BBC in Manchester. Then, after he had made a documentary about alligators and dolphins in China, in 1985 Anglia's wildlife series *Survival* invited him to film the giant anaconda in South America.

"I went into the tropical rainforest for the first time, and that was it," he later recalled. "I simply fell in love with the heat, the humidity, the snakes, the insects, the animals, the natives. I knew I couldn't leave it. I was a Rainforest Man."

Gordon explored deep into the Amazon basin, where there were no white men and only the occasional Brazilian river trader; he made a clearing in the jungle and built a house out of fallen timber, where he would live for up to ten months at a time.

Gordon worked for *Survival* for some 15 years; apart from ITV, his films appeared on Channel 4, the BBC and the National Geographic channel; they were shown in more than 100 countries.

He is best known for *Jaguar – Eater of Souls* (ITV, 2001), the result of seven years filming the life of one of the world's most elusive big cats. To make it, he needed to earn the trust of the peoples who shared the jaguar's world, particularly the Yanamami and the Matis.

On one occasion, when he was visiting a Yanamami village, Gordon's hosts tried to persuade him to sample the local narcotic, *yoppo*; when he refused, they imprisoned him in the longhouse. "We escaped, and hid in the jungle until they had gone off to massacre a neighbouring tribe," he said.

Other documentaries made by Gordon included: *Creatures of the Magic Water* (1995), about the animals found around an Amazonian creek; *Web of the Spider Monkey* (1996); and *Gremlins: Faces in the Forest* (1998), about marmosets. In order to build three filming towers for the programme about spider monkeys, he shipped 10 tonnes of scaffolding from Britain to Brazil, then had it moved by canoe to the site in the jungle.

Gordon rescued and cared for a number of orphaned animals, including two jaguar cubs which he gave to a wildlife reserve in the region when they became too dangerous to look after.

He was the author of two books: *Tarantulas, Marmosets and other Stories* (1997) and *In the Heart of the Amazon* (2002).

Gordon was filming a new seven-part series, *Secrets of the Amazon*, when he died on April 25, apparently from a heart attack, on the border between Venezuela and Brazil.

He is survived by his second wife, Antonieta Cavalcante, who worked as his assistant and interpreter, and by a daughter from his first marriage.

Reproduced by kind permission of the *Daily Telegraph*

Opposite: **Close encounter – the jaguar is fascinated by its own reflection in Nick's lens**

Where are they?

1

2

3

Places where I
encountered some
of the birds and
animals

6

4

5

6

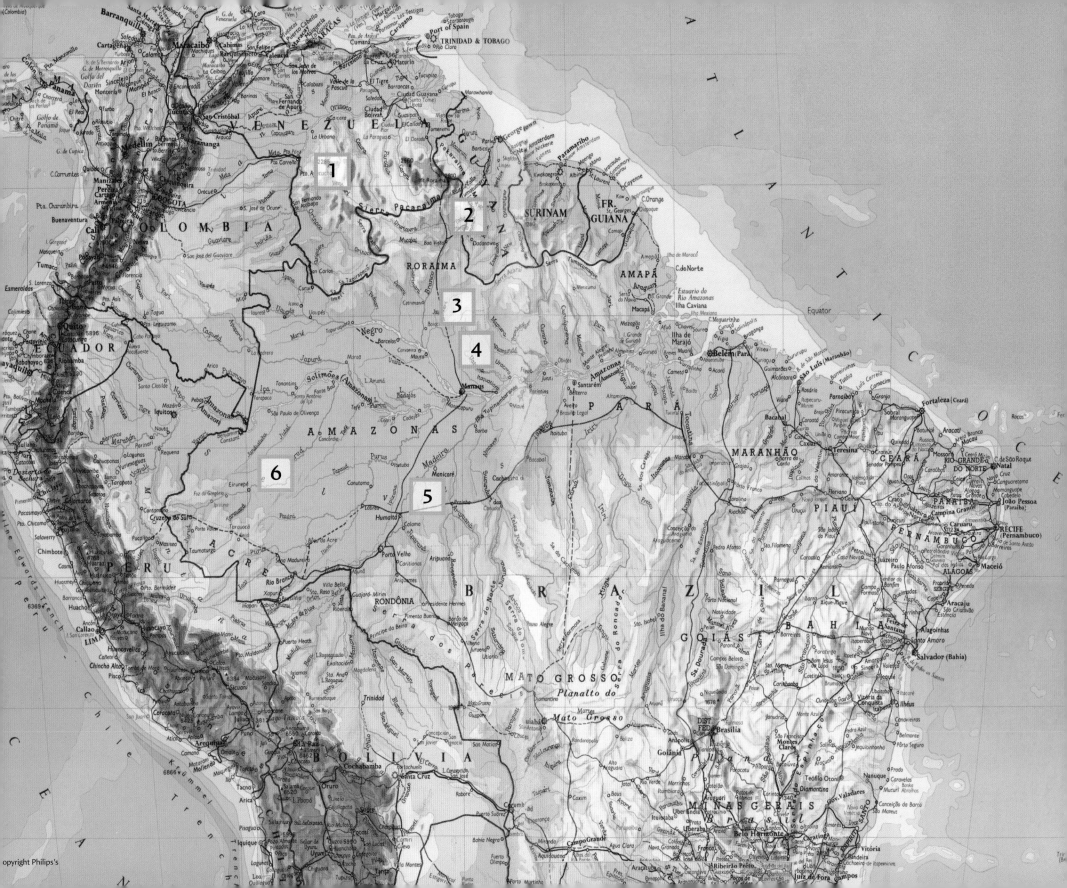

Green Hell – The Myth

"All the pictures my imagination had painted in anticipation of the impression of a virgin forest would make on me sank like faded shadows into insignificance before the sublime reality that discloses itself on entering it!"

Richard Schomburgk
'Travels in British Guiana', *Daily Chronicle*, Georgetown, 1922

The Amazonian rainforest has fascinated me for almost as long as I can remember. Even as a young boy, I was enthralled by adventurous tales such as Conan Doyle's *Lost World*, in which the fictional hero Professor Challenger and his companions discover a mountain, cut off from the jungles below, inhabited by creatures believed to be long extinct.

On the other hand, real-life explorer Colonel Percy Fawcett's purportedly true accounts of 62-feet-long Amazonian anacondas confused me. Why would a man who has come across something so fantastic pull out his revolver and smash '... a .44 soft-nosed bullet into its spine, ten feet below the wicked head'? Of course, the answer to that question lies within the subtext of other quotes from his expedition: '...vampire bats were also a nuisance... their [the men's] hammocks saturated with blood... snakes were always a constant threat... they were attacked by a seven-foot bushmaster... put two slugs through the ugly head of the creature...' This was a story-bound Green Hell that I would one day discover bore no resemblance to the natural paradise that is Amazonia.

Subconsciously, even at that age, I must have realised it was all tosh, because I couldn't believe a 'real' explorer would go about killing such interesting creatures. And why were snakes heads ugly? I thought they were terrific. Wildlife fascinated me and the foothills and cliffs of the Berwyn Mountains in North Wales, close to my school, became my very own *Lost World*. My friend Brian and I mounted our own expeditions to find adders and grass snakes; we scaled the local crags just to peep at a kestrel's nest and I felt every bit as intrepid as Fawcett was made out to be.

By the age of thirteen I had, fortunately, moved on to rather more informed and trustworthy books. Henry Walter Bates' incomparable *The Naturalist on the Amazons* became my favourite. His personal account of living there for eleven years in the 1850s was fascinating and, eventually, a valuable research tool. The region is not, as more fanciful accounts would have us believe, a 'green hell', an impenetrable mass in which dangers lurk at every twist and turn. It is, in fact, one immense living, breathing organism thatharbours the least understood ecosystem on our planet.

Amazonia is, quite simply, the greatest rainforest on earth. It covers over 2.25 million square miles (4 million square kilometres) of land, crossing the political borders of nine countries. During the rain season, one-fifth of all fresh water on our planet eventually flows along the largest river, the Amazon, which pours into the Atlantic Ocean at 45 million gallons (more than 200 million litres) per second. The ocean water is affected more than 90 miles (150 kilometres) out to sea!

Almost half the world's undisturbed tropical evergreen forest is found here, and it boasts some 50 per cent of the world's terrestrial species, including rare – and often unique – animals and plants. Over a quarter of all prescription medicines originate here, and some of the discoveries made here have affected countless millions of people – yet to date, less than two per cent of the plants have been studied.

This powerhouse of biodiversity is also home to forest-dwelling Amerindian cultures, some of which, even in this twenty-first century, have still not been contacted by the 'outside' world.

My first face-to-face encounter with the rainforest came in 1987, when Anglia Television's world-famous natural history film unit, *Survival*, commissioned me to make a series of one-hour television specials in the northern area of Amazonia. 'The forest teems with wildlife,' my synopsis told me. 'Watch where you step,' a close friend (clearly a Percy Fawcett convert) said when we bid each other farewell in London.

Opposite: A real-life "Lost World" – Wahari Kuawai, a mountain sacred to the Piaroa Indians of northern Amazonia

"My filming ambitions were fired
from the moment I first walked into

Guyana's virgin rainforest.

I genuinely felt an overpowering awareness of my own insignificance
that moved me in a way that
I had never experienced before."

But finally standing there, taking in the eerie silence, the hugeness of the trees, I started to panic – it was so dark! Would there be enough light to film? Where was that teeming wildlife? The only creatures I could see were the ants swarming over my boots and crawling up my legs. I obviously needed to understand the real meaning of biodiversity.

My loathing of the 'Green Hell' premise was born as I realised that this was nothing like the fictional, threatening land that Percy and others had written of; it couldn't be! Branches crashed above me, one almost scoring a direct hit with my head, but I couldn't see what had caused the commotion. Subtle signs pointed to where a snake had shed its skin and I did get stung by some tiny wasps, but these things just reinforced the fact that one had to understand this forest to enjoy its secrets. I had never been so excited in my life.

My local Macusi guide pointed out animal tracks on the edge of the Rupununi River. He told me that a jaguar had made them. Even before my professional career had begun I knew that, in wildlife film making, capturing a wild jaguar on film was considered the equivalent of achieving the Holy Grail.

I lived in Guyana for two years, filming giant otters for my first television special, before moving 500 miles (800 kilometres) south to start my next film project. It was there, just before dawn on a December morning in 1992, that something happened that would change the course of my life.

It was 5.30 a.m. and I was shivering. Considering this was the equator, it was surprisingly cold. Holed up in a large pit on a sandbank in the upper Rio Branco in northern Brazil, I was trying to film the giant expansa terrapins that nest there at that time of year. I had been told that jaguars came here to catch the huge creatures, but in three exhausting days and nights I had seen only black vultures. I was watching these avian undertakers squabble over some uncovered terrapin eggs when the atmosphere suddenly changed. Twenty or more vultures flapped urgently into the air and wheeled away to the treetops at the forest edge close by. Every hair on my body tingled.

Then I saw her: a wild jaguar. This was no fraction-of-a-second glimpse obscured by tangled vegetation. Just 65 yards (60 metres) away, with nothing between us but smooth white sand, the most glorious cat was walking straight towards me.

I felt no fear – just immense frustration as I realised that, typically, my camera was out of film. About 100 feet (30 metres) in front of me, the jaguar stopped and stared for one long minute, before sauntering back into the forest. What a shot that would have been! An hour later she reappeared at the forest edge, but only briefly – then she disappeared for ever. I spent three more months there and never saw her again.

That experience was the spark that ignited a passionate affair with a forest that would keep me within its grasp for the next decade. It would be a slow process of discovery and learning, but one that was obviously going to be endlessly fascinating. In the fullness of time I would achieve my jaguar film, but there were other equally absorbing challenges ahead.

Living in Amazonia for almost fifteen years, I came to know the forest, its people and its animals intimately. Despite serious illness and some truly terrifying moments, usually brought about by my own stupidity, I wish I could spend several lifetimes filming and learning there.

Even then, I would still understand only a fraction of its complexity.

My youngest daughter, Emma, was just eight years old when she first visited my Amazon forest camp. Even at her tender age, she was aware of and concerned about the encroaching threats of deforestation. Sitting on my lap 140 feet (40 metres) up on top of one of my filming towers, we were gazing out across the sea of unbroken trees when she asked me if I was going to save the rainforest.

I told her that I just wanted my films to make people who could make a difference aware of how beautiful and precious the forest is. 'But they go down the tv tube in just one hour, Dad,' she said. 'Why don't you make a photography book that lasts longer?'

This book is the result of that conversation. It brings together some of my best photographs and most unforgettable experiences. I can only hope that it succeeds in revealing the wonder and diversity of life in what is probably the last remaining true wilderness on Earth.

Nick Gordon

Nick Gordon

Opposite: **An early encounter with a wild jaguar**

CHAPTER 1

Eater of Souls

"... the jaguars prowled at night... so like a shadow moving that when I examined the place, and saw nothing, it was easy to believe the eye was only suspicious"

Henry Major Tomlinson
The Sea and the Jungle (1912)

At our feet, on the bare earth floor of the communal hut, sat a large jaguar's skull. Squatting around it were three Matis Indians, preparing their lethal blow darts for the four days' hunting ahead, their faces pierced with spines to mimic whiskers which, together with their ear ornaments, made them look like pantomime cats. As I filmed, clouds of small, biting black flies filled my eyes, ears and nose, making life almost unbearable. In broken Portuguese, the Matis chief Bina explained how a fellow tribesman had tracked down the jaguar and killed it with arrows a few weeks earlier. Before I had the chance to ask him why, Bina said simply: 'It ate one of us'.

It was 9 March 1998. With my camera assistant, Neil Shaw, I had travelled to the Javari Valley, one of the most remote areas in Amazonia, more than 300 miles (500 kilometres) along the Itui River from Tabatinga on the Brazilian-Colombian border. We were here to film the Jaguar People, as I had come to know the Matis – a people whose reverence for the jaguar as the forest's supreme hunter is the foundation of their way of life. Like all forest people, they treat the big cat with deep respect born of tremendous fear. This was the culmination

of a dream I had nursed for almost ten years: to film one of the world's most elusive wild creatures, *Panthera onça* – the jaguar. During the 1970s, despite the region's isolation, outsiders desperate to extract as much valuable timber and mineral wealth from the rainforest as possible discovered the valley. Those 'invaders' came into direct contact with the Matis and passed on a virulent flu virus to which the Indians had no resistance. Within one year, their community of 240 people was devastated. Only 50 people survived it. With a potentially unviable population, the Matis were facing the dreadful possibility of extinction. Tragically, too, the jaguar that they so revere was also facing extermination. The skin trade's ugly fingers had reached into the remotest corners of this land. Countless thousands of jaguars were wiped out for their glorious coats.

In an ironic twist, the Matis were saved by the outsiders' modern medicines. The Matis population is slowly recovering, and currently stands at 125. The jaguars' reprieve came from international legislation prohibiting trade in their skins. Latest official estimates of their numbers vary between 10,000 and 15,000 so today they, too, seem to be faring better – at least in the Javari Valley.

Opposite: All Matis men (and boys) are hunters. Here they prepare the poison on the tips of their darts

Jaguars are impossible to follow in the wild with a camera. They are loners, shy hunters who avoid humans, for good reason. All we know about them has been gathered from a very few field studies, done with trapped and radio-collared individuals, and by observations of captive animals. What is certain is that they have the most powerful jaws in the cat world and are the only big cats to regularly kill prey by piercing the skull with their canines.

My research data told me that four other species of the Felidae or cat family live here. The puma (*Puma concolor*) is equally at home in this rainforest as it is in the mountainous wilds of Chile or even Canada. In Portuguese it is called *onça vehmelho*, or red jaguar, but it really is a lightweight compared to the jaguar.

The jaguarundi – *Felis (Herpailurus) yagouaroundi*, – like the puma, has a plain spotless coat, but is darker coloured and much smaller. About the size of a large house cat, it is very sleek and has a head shaped more like that of an otter than a cat (in fact, in some places it is known as the

otter cat). Finally, there are the two smaller spotted species, the margay (*Felis wiedii*) and the ocelot (*Felis pardalis*). The ocelot is predominantly a ground hunter, whereas the margay is superbly skilled at hunting up in the trees. In my opinion, it is the most elegant of all the Amazonian cats.

Of all the Amazonian cats, jaguars have by far the largest territories – up to 100 square miles (160 square kilometres) for a male – and coming across wild jaguars, even for the Indians who live in the forest, is rare. This highlighted one of our major problems. So little is known about jaguars' life in the wild that most of their natural behaviour remains a mystery. For example, I had read that jaguars often rest on boughs that overhang creeks, waiting for prey to happen by, but I had never thought of them as good climbers like African leopards. Then, during our first stay with the Matis Indians, we witnessed a remarkable sight. Far from the riverside village, as we were filming army ants on the forest floor, Neil pointed to a movement high up in a tree some distance away. Looking through the binoculars, we

could see that it was a big opossum, which for some reason had left its daytime resting place. A few seconds later, we heard something large and heavy rushing through the undergrowth.

Trembling with excitement, I whipped the camera around on its tripod and focused halfway up the tree as the silhouette of a large cat climbed up it at incredible speed. The opossum had obviously seen the danger coming, because it raced along a thin branch and into the crown of the next tree. Clinging to the tree trunk about 65 feet (20 metres) up, the jaguar realised it had lost its meal and began to slide down, using its front paws and claws to hug the tree and keep from falling. We lost sight of it behind the lower level of vegetation and, only then, wondered nervously if it might come our way. We waited in silence, our hearts thumping, for what seemed like an eternity but couldn't hear any sound of it. Eventually, we moved towards the tree, deliberately making a lot of noise. All that was left to show that the cat had been there was thick white sap dripping from the bark where its claws had cut into the wood.

Above: **Jaguarundi, nocturnal margay cats and ocelot**

Above: **A previously unknown phenomenon – a jaguar climbing a tree**

The Jaguar People

Gaining the trust and respect of the people was, more often than not, a drawn-out and delicate affair. It can be difficult to keep a low profile when you are the continual object of curiosity. Trying to understand our presence from their point of view was vital if our stay was to be safe and harmonious. It didn't always work out, of course; after all, we are all only human.

Concepts of privacy or possession simply don't exist. The community's survival naturally depends upon everyone sharing everything. Initially, this was a source of potential conflict and had to be handled extremely carefully.

Generally, after one week we would be able to mix freely with them and it was amazing how we learnt to communicate with them using just body language. There were occasions when we felt vulnerable, but rarely were we frightened for our lives. Our first encounter with the Matis, however, made me shake with fear.

We had not seen a single human being for two and a half days when we spotted two canoes ahead. Four Matis men were paddling across the river in front of us: we had reached the Jaguar People's village. I was still in a state of near apoplexy at that first sight of them as we climbed the mud slope to their community. I heard the grunting first and looked nervously at my companions. Instinctively, we drew closer together.

From the forest tree line, at the edge of the village, a human wall of Matis warriors emerged. Their faces and naked torsos were covered with grey mud. Wearing some kind of palm leaves around their waists, all of them were making deep guttural grunts as they stamped their feet raising dust, quickly moving towards us. It was so

menacing. Eventually we discovered it was a pre-hunt ritual called Dance of the Peccary, but I do wonder to this day if it had been intentionally scary – or simply an indigenous leg-pull.

Living in any of the remote forest communities is extremely difficult for us outsiders. Used to our sanitised and pampered way of life, it is hard to imagine a more extraordinary, uncomfortable or unhealthy existence than theirs. Once they were accustomed to our living among them, I could handle being constantly stared at and followed, even going into the forest to defecate. I could deal with twenty or more Matis in the hut sifting through our bags and cases. But I never came to terms with the black fly. Despite the constant village din during the daytime, mainly from women screaming at men and the incessant barking of dogs, if you closed your eyes and just listened, one sound emerged above all others: hands slapping flesh.

In West Africa this same tiny fly is the very scourge of life. It carries the disease onchocerciasis, commonly called river blindness. For some inexplicable reason, although the disease does exist here, it has not run rampant through this forest's human population. But even so, the black fly makes life a misery. Wherever you stop along the river, the dreadful things descend upon you immediately and suck your blood.

This would not be so bad if their bites didn't leave the most dreadful itch you can imagine. In the Javari Valley, the Matis village suffers the same fate. The bodies of everyone who lives there are covered from head to toe in tiny blood specks where the flies have bitten. Arms and hands constantly flay their chests, tummies, backs,

"From the forest tree line, at the edge of the village, a human wall of Matis warriors emerged. Their faces and naked torsos were covered with grey mud. Wearing some kind of palm leaves around their waists, all of them were making deep guttural grunts as they stamped their feet raising dust, quickly moving towards us. It was so menacing."

arms and legs, smacking the little devils after they have bitten. The only time I ever witnessed humour regarding the fly's presence was when Makur, a hunter, was bitten on his penis and misjudged a swipe with his hand. His painful expletives reduced everyone within earshot to tears of laughter.

All men are hunters, until they become too old. From the time they learn to walk, boys carry miniature bows and arrows. They are toys with a vital purpose, and only the boys use them. Makur was one of the Matis' most respected hunters and, for some unfathomable reason, he took a curious interest in my camera and me. Gone was the initial wariness and reticence when he led me into the *molluca*, or communal hut, five days after our arrival, to show me his preparations for the hunt ahead.

The molluca was a massive thatched construction, some 130 feet (40 metres) long, 65 feet (20 metres) wide and 50 feet (15 metres) high. Twenty-three families lived in it, each with their own patch for their hammocks and a fire. Smoke constantly drifted up into the roof, blackening the thatch and slowly seeping away. The air was thick and caught the back of my throat. It was too dark to see until our eyes adjusted, and then we could make out people, their faces decorated like cats, staring at us from the shadows.

Just inside the small entrance two men were whittling blow darts from palm frond spines. A small boy was squeezing the fly bites on the back of one of the men. Makur squatted next to them. He picked up a small gourd and, using a little stick, scraped some thick, black tar-like substance from it. On a small wooden dish he mixed it with a few drops of river water and stirred it into a paste. This was curare, the toxic substance they paint their dart and arrowheads with.

Curare (*Curarea toxifera*) is made from the bark of a vine. Its early history is largely obscure although it is known that forest Indians have used it for hundreds of years. It's a powerful muscle relaxant that can drop a heavy monkey from the treetops in seconds. First knowledge of it came to Europe from Sir Walter Raleigh, who brought news of its existence to Queen Elizabeth 1.

During the 1800s various experiments were carried out using curare and at the turn of the twentieth century, Rudolf Boehm of Leipzig University produced Curarin, the synthetic equivalent commonly used as an anaesthetic worldwide today. I often wonder what other medical miracles exist in the forest – or, because of man's stupidity and greed, have been lost before we have even had a chance to discover them.

The whole community was becoming excited by the prospect of the hunt. They knew that in a few days the men would return with a lot of fresh meat – a vital boost of protein for them. Even the smallest children were more animated than usual, running about mimicking the hunters firing bows or using blow pipes, but one morning their good mood suddenly changed.

There are times, when we are living among native communities, when it is extremely difficult to hide our own emotions. Bina, the Matis chief, had called us from our hut where we were cleaning camera equipment. (Earlier that morning, much to everyone's hilarity except my own, a mangy dog had urinated all over my £50,000 film camera.) He motioned for me to follow him,

saying in Portuguese, 'the spirits of the forest are here, come.'

He led us to the communal hut and told us to sit in one corner and, putting a finger to his mouth, he made a hush gesture. I wondered where he had learnt that. Most of the Matis men who had not gone hunting, about twenty of them, and many women were there, all of them silent. Through the low entrance three grotesque figures appeared. Like living bushes of vegetation, they waddled exaggeratedly in a squatting position. Their faces were hideous pottery masks, and their bodies were painted black. Their hands gripped 13-foot- (4-metre)-long, flexible whips carved from palm fronds.

A tiny child, no more than four years old was dragged into the hut, screaming hysterically. Secured by a man he was pulled in front of the spirits. They were chanting incoherently and the women present began to shout in high-pitched tones. The palm frond whips sliced through the air and curled around the small child's waist. Red welts appeared almost immediately. As he screamed again, the palm whips flayed a second time – then he was released in a panic-stricken state. The Matis were clearly amused by the ceremony. Neil couldn't watch any more and left the hut; it was too upsetting for him.

This rite, the chief told me, was a punishment for disobedience meted out by the forest's spirits to their children just once every year. I hadn't thought about it up to that point in time but I realised then that I had never seen a Matis man or woman chastise any child. For one hour child after child was manhandled to face the agony. I eventually moved outside and sat on the

bare earth opposite the hut. After a while the three spirit figures appeared and positioned themselves either side of the doorway; it obviously wasn't over yet. The final obstacle for the kids was getting out of the place. As they fled from the hut, the spirits again tried to thrash them. I asked Bina if I could take some pictures of the forest spirits and he said yes, as long as they were not shown 'teaching' the children. This was not a reference to showing them in any negative kind of way but, he told me, because they believed that the spirits' power would be reduced.

During our first week there, all of our food supplies had been taken. This presented us with a serious concern, as we would have to rely on our hosts for provisions. Our foreign digestive systems are, compared to the Matis, delicate and prone to bacterial infections while they of course have resistance. Now, it seemed, the approaching hunt was going to be as important to us as it would be for them.

At dawn on the day the men were to leave for the hunt, Makur and two women were sitting outside the side entrance to the communal hut. Between them some smouldering fire embers were being fanned as a third man arrived and handed

a huge bright green tree frog to Makur. The previous year we had filmed this wonderfully large nocturnal frog, as big as my hand, mating in the forest next to our camp. Its common name is the monkey frog (*Phyllomedusa bicolor*). The chorus of the males as they try to attract a female is a very impressive sound in the dead of night.

Makur had put four short sticks into the ground at the corner of a tiny smoking fire. He used strips of palm leaf to secure the frog's limbs, which he then gently stretched out and tied to the sticks. The frog began to ooze a thick whitish liquid from its skin – a highly toxic defence mechanism. One woman gently scraped the toxin off and put it on a small piece of wood while her companion concentrated on burning the end of a stick in the fire.

As the frog was untied and released – seemingly none the worse for its ordeal – the burning stick was pulled out of the fire. The woman blew on the end, extinguishing the flame, and then stabbed Makur in his right bicep with it. He winced and uttered something, but smiled at me. The two women hooted with laughter.

One of them dabbed a drop of the frog toxin onto the open wound. The same was done

Opposite: **Matis spirits of the forest; they terrify the children.** Above: **Makur scraping toxin from the monkey frog**

to the second man who had provided the frog. Within seconds, both looked pale and ill. Several women now arrived carrying huge pots of water from the river. As they continually doused the men with water, to keep their body temperature down, Makur and the other man started projectile vomiting. Thirty minutes later they were moaning, retching and unable to stand. One hour later they sat in a trance-like state, eyes unfocused and staring wildly.

Bina explained to me that this ritual was to clear the hunters' bodies and minds of food and liquid, which would sharpen their physical and spiritual senses while they hunted. In this heightened state of awareness, they would be much more alert to prey and danger. It was at times like this that I used to realise just how fundamentally different two human beings could be. Although Makur and I were a similar age and, in one sense, lived in the same world, we might as well have come from different planets. Makur was going out to get food from his forest, a necessity for him as normal as brushing my teeth is for me. Yet if we were to swap environments, he would survive the change whereas I most certainly would not. It was always a humbling thought.

With the men away hunting, the village seemed unnaturally quiet; even the normally infuriating dogs and chickens seemed subdued. That all changed early one morning, five days after the men had set out. Children and women ran past us towards the river: the men were back.

Five canoes were pulled onto the dried mud at the river's edge and fifteen men, all smiling, came up the hill. They carried eight dead spider and woolly monkeys, all fully grown adults. The kids touched them as they ran and skipped

alongside the men. Wild pig and deer, a favourite food, had also been killed and were being carried over the hill, shouldered by young men. A mood of feast and celebration infected everyone. That night in the communal hut many different families prepared the banquet. It was a gruesome sight to our eyes. Large bowls were filled with what looked like dead human babies; primates' hands and arms protruded from the cloudy, boiling water. I told Neil that there was no way I could eat spider monkey – it would be like eating Pete, my pet monkey at the time – but he was so hungry he would try anything.

Above: **Matis hunting ritual – the Dance of the Peccary.** Above right: **As the frog toxin circulates in his body, Makur is cooled down with water**

Above: **The giant monkey frog, which is only active at night**

"The massive head turned and **snarled** at us.
It was so close
I could have touched it with the paddle.
As we sat in the boat, sick and awestruck,
he disappeared into the forest
without so much as a backward glance."

That, it turned out, was his downfall. I was suffering from malaria, but Neil had become seriously ill, with what turned out to be an ulcerated intestine. I needed to get him to hospital as quickly as possible. Tabatinga was three days' away along the Itui River, and so we organised a boat journey and made ourselves as comfortable as we could. Frustrated and disappointed after just two weeks with the Matis, we had to leave.

The river was flanked by tall forest for most of the journey back. Apart from bird life, there was little else to look at until our second afternoon afloat. Then our boatman, Didi, pointed to something in the water some 220 yards (200 metres) ahead. 'Capybara,' he said confidently. Through the binoculars, I could already see that he was wrong.

The Itui was about 550 yards (500 metres) wide at this point, and the jaguar was only halfway across. As we approached it, I asked Didi not to get too close but he ignored me. The massive head turned and snarled at us. It was so close I could have touched it with the paddle. Despite our presence, the jaguar's powerful swimming rhythm didn't change at all. The current bobbed us away from him, and we watched as he reached the riverbank. He clambered into a thick tangle of branches, and then shook the water off himself. He was a big cat; an adult male can weigh 330 pounds (150 kilograms), and this one must have been close to that. As we sat in the boat, sick and awestruck, he disappeared into the forest without so much as a backward glance.

Above left: **Poison dart or arrow frogs, traditionally used by some forest Indians to obtain toxins to tip their blow darts and arrows.**
Centre and right: **Matis men are skilled hunters with blowpipes. They are used mainly on birds and monkeys**

Above: **Facial ornaments that mimic the jaguar are worn by the Matis every day; their skin is pierced when they are tiny children**

Spirit of the Jaguar

My first encounter with one of these magnificent cats on the Rio Branco sandbanks was now seven years ago, but it was that first face-to-face meeting that had convinced me to set up a permanent camp in the Amazon forest. From there I was well placed to reach the farthest and most remote corners of Amazonia, and I never missed an opportunity to follow up leads of good jaguar sightings. Neil and I made three journeys to the spectacular mountain range that forms the political border with Venezuela. This is Yanomami Indian territory – and jaguar country, too.

The jaguar is at the very heart of the Yanomami religion – they call it Iraruie, the 'Eater of Souls', in the belief that the jaguar's spirit consumes the souls of their dead. Traditionally the Yanomami do not use medicines because, they believe, all diseases come from spiritual causes. When a person is dying, Iraruie is the last spirit to leave the body because he is the only one strong enough to fight to the last minute. So tribal shamen call upon the jaguar's spirit to cure the sick and dying.

Yanomami people call their spirits Hekura. The jaguar, or Hekura Iraruie, is the cornerstone of their world and is responsible for sheltering all of the other Hekura. There are several different types of Hekura; many are associated with forest animals but some are purely elemental. The sun, moon, lightning and thunder are powerful Hekura and interestingly the moon, Periporuie, is very important and considered almost evil.

One afternoon during our first week with the Yanomami we heard some strange cries coming from behind our hut. I wandered outside to find an amazing scene. Several village elders were squatting together, blasting hallucinogenic powder, through 3-foot- (1-metre)-long wooden tubes, up each other's noses. Behind them the shaman was strutting and dancing in the centre of a clearing between the huts. With dramatic thrusts of his arms, he mimicked lightning strikes and called out for Iraruie to awaken. Towering dramatically behind the village and forest were the mountains of the Sierra de Neblina. This, the shaman told me, is where Iraruie lived. He also added that the Hekura could sometimes be bad. I shivered for a second.

The Yanomami we met during this first expedition told us they had lost one of their men to a jaguar just a few months earlier. With the Matis experience, these were the only believable instances I ever heard of a jaguar killing and eating a human. While most hunters have numerous tales of close encounters with them at one time or another, it's obvious that such attacks are very much the exception – though they do make entertaining stories during the long nights in the rainforest!

Several times each year the Yanomami men, like the Matis, trek far from their village on extended hunts. They build temporary camps in the forest from where they track monkey, deer and peccary, the most prized food sources. It was a real privilege to be invited to accompany one of these expeditions. They always hunt alone, but two of them agreed to show me an area where they said there were caves and, more importantly, regular jaguar sightings. We rose before dawn, and by 6 a.m. we were deep in the forest, overshadowed by towering rock formations. Suddenly, one of the Indians pointed to the ground: there was a pile of jaguar faeces, and sticking out of it were the unmistakeable hooked claws of a sloth. There was no doubt that we were close – the spoor was fresh.

Both our guides seemed nervous as we came to a sandy area in front of the rocks. We struggled up onto a boulder the size of a bungalow and looked about. After a few minutes, one of the Yanomami muttered to his companion, and they moved off towards the nearest cave entrance, with us following closely behind. A small, shallow creek ran from within the cave and cut through the rocks to our right. Then, in the soft, damp sand at our feet, we saw the proof we needed: cat prints going into and coming out of the cave, smaller paw-marks mixed in with large ones.

None of us wanted to hang around the entrance – a female jaguar with young can be very dangerous. We moved back behind the boulders and found a place about 100 feet (30 metres) away where we could just see the cave entrance. One of the men patiently sharpened his lethal-looking spear-like arrowheads. I looked on, entranced, thinking that there was no way those arrows would stop a charging eater of souls in its tracks. Five humid hours later we were still there, having heard and seen nothing. But I thought it would be worthwhile spending another full day there, to film the scenery if nothing else, and so we returned at dawn the next day.

I have no doubt that the four of us experienced the adrenaline rush at precisely the same moment. I saw the two cubs first. They tumbled across the small rocks at the water's edge, play-fighting, and then disappeared into the cave. Seconds later, the mother's head appeared around the side of a rock. She was utterly magnificent, her markings vivid black rosettes on pure gold. She dipped her head, sniffed the ground and then moved into the cave. The whole event probably only lasted 30 seconds, but it seemed to pass in slow motion. Neil and I looked at each other, both wide-eyed and open-mouthed in amazement.

Jaguar cubs are born blind, and their eyes open after about two weeks. Judging by the way these two were moving around, I guessed they were about 12 weeks old and probably beginning to make hunting more difficult for their mother. Or would they have the instinct to lie low if she spotted prey?

Our distant and varied travels with the Matis and Yanomami peoples were priceless once-in-a-lifetime experiences that I will never forget. My quest to make a film about the jaguar had kept me firmly anchored to the rainforest floor but, as I had learnt from my first foray into this rainforest, most life remained well out of reach 130–160 feet (40–50 metres) above the ground. The forest canopy was to be my next great challenge.

Opposite and above: **Like all young cats, jaguar cubs are constantly playing and exploring the world around them**

CHAPTER 2

An Ocean of Trees

"The forest; wife of silence, mother of solitude... the cathedral where unknown gods speak in low, mumbling voices, promising long life to the awe-inspiring trees as old as the heavens and ancient when the first tribes appeared..."

José Eustasio Rivera
Colombian author and poet (1889–1928)

Nothing can prepare your mind for that very first experience of leaving the ground behind and travelling up into the roof of the rainforest. Phil Hurrell, a friend and colleague from the BBC Natural History Unit in Bristol, England, had devoted a lot of time and energy to designing a safe and relatively portable means of getting Sir David Attenborough up into the rainforest canopy on a previous project. Over a pint in a Bristol pub, I told him that I wanted not just to get up there but also to be able to film the journey up and down – and more! He smiled wryly at my cameraman's imagination running riot as I described the perfect, steady, moving shots that I wanted to capture. Even though he hadn't seen my Amazon camp at that time, he knew better than anyone, including me, what the limitations were and the logistics involved. But get me up there he did and, thanks to him, I captured what had been, up to that point, merely my dream 'wish-list' shots, and much more besides.

In simple terms, Phil's contraption was a basic counterbalance system with a huge bag filled with sand on one end and a bosun's chair on the other, where I would sit with my camera. We had to fix pulleys, webbing straps, shackles and mountaineering devices to the trees and ropes and, of course, there were miles of cables to secure everything twice, just to be extra sure – it's a long drop. We also had to get the balance of weight perfect or, as he told me, one of two things would happen: I would either take off like a missile and cover some 130 feet (40 metres) in just a few seconds, or my helpers would have to haul me skywards with great difficulty and then, with them unable to support my weight, I would plummet to the earth at 22 feet (6.5 metres) per second squared. After several nervous trials, we eventually got it right and a whole new world came into view for the first time.

Rising in slow motion from the forest floor to the treetops that day was one of my life's never-to-be-forgotten moments. At last I could see clearly the forest's architecture. What appears from the ground to be a confusion of vegetation clearly divides into different, separate layers or zones. Above the floor and the lowest vegetation, you enter the void of a middle layer or storey before entering the lower canopy trees. Finally, you reach the rooftop and gaze out across a spectacular green ocean.

Opposite: Trees as far as the eye can see: this is where the Equator crosses Amazonia. Above: A lone flowering tree. Trees of the same species flower at the same time and yet the nearest relative to this one was more than half a mile (1 kilometre) away – the visual proof of biodiversity

My static, scaffold filming towers were invaluable in their own way, but this new added dimension of mobility was stunning. What struck me immediately was the number of plants growing on others. These are mostly epiphytes and some recent studies have found over one hundred species on just one tree. A parasitic plant, like the mistletoe, actually drains its host of sustenance, but an epiphyte uses its host purely for support. Just 50 feet (15 metres) above the forest floor, they covered almost every surface that I could see, even many leaves. But how did they get up here in the first place?

It's surprisingly windy at times in this upper layer of the forest and many epiphyte seeds find their place to take root having been swept through the tree crowns on air currents. Others get a free ride in the guts of birds, bats, monkeys and other animals, until they are passed out in their droppings, some of which inevitably stick to the surfaces of branches, tree trunks and foliage. Here they can germinate in their own free packets of fertiliser.

Despite this being one of the wettest regions of the world, the plants up here have to survive prolonged periods under the fierce tropical sun, without water. Many epiphytes have evolved thick, waxy foliage to cut down water loss and some ingenious ways of making the most of what moisture is available.

My favourite epiphytes were the bromeliads and orchids and I spent many happy hours pushing my close-up macro lenses into them, trying to capture their hidden secrets – although the first bromeliad that I investigated closely gave me a bit of a start. As I gently moved

"After several nervous trials, we eventually got it right and a whole new world came into view for the first time... and I gazed out across a spectacular green ocean."

the stiff, sharp-edged leaves apart, a perfectly camouflaged 2-foot- (60-cm) -long parrot snake slithered out and across my wrist. I resolved to look carefully before I touched anything in future…

Bromeliads have thick, coarse spiky leaves that overlap at the bottom of the plant. These act as rainwater gutters that channel water to the base and form a very effective storage reservoir. This high-altitude water supply has not been overlooked by the myriad creatures that live here, and many tiny creatures pass their entire lives in these pond plants. The larvae of insects develop here; tadpoles, too. The dreaded mosquito that had so blighted my life here breeds in the still water, and leaves that fall and snag in the bromeliads drop into the wet trough and slowly decompose. The nourishing mulch that they produce attracts feeding snails, beetles and other flying insects. These attract lizards and arboreal frogs, and these in turn, snakes.

Above: **My tallest filming tower – 167 feet (52 metres) high and more than two tons in weight**

Above: The *Philodendron*, an epiphyte whose succulent-looking fruit is laced with oxalic acid

Generally, epiphytes such as the bromeliads and orchids only need to put down roots to anchor themselves to the surface of their support host, whether it's a leaf, branch or a tree trunk. But there are other epiphytes that produce true aerial roots. These grow until they reach the forest floor about 100 feet (30 metres) or more below, where they creep beneath the leaf litter and begin to tap the supply of food and water there. One of the first examples of this that I decided to film was a *Philodendron*. It was a huge plant with twenty or more large leaves, which at that time had produced fruit. Dropping vertically to the floor hidden from me were five aerial roots, each one half an inch (1 cm) thick.

One dawn I captured a remarkable piece of behaviour on film. A family of spider monkeys had come into the crown of the host tree. They investigated the *Philodendron*'s amber yellow fruit, about the size of a large courgette. Four of them took it in turns to eat many of the small fruitlets that covered it, swallowing them without chewing. The *Philodendron* protects its seeds with a powerful concentration of oxalic acid which masticating animals would find very unpalatable, or even choke on.

More fascinating than this was the behaviour of two of the spider monkeys who had turned their attention to the aerial roots. With their superbly long, prehensile tails anchored around a branch, they pulled up the roots, arm over arm, until the tips of them were in their hands. Then they fed on the juicy green growth.

Above: **Spider monkeys love nectar, too!**

On that first memorable voyage into the canopy, the second thing that I realised was that when you crane your neck and look up from the forest floor, you simply can't see 90 per cent of what is actually growing up here, or indeed going on. I had always found it easy to enthuse about the fauna of the rainforest, but due to my lack of knowledge had never thought of the flora in the same way. That quickly changed as I came to see, learn and understand more about what some biologists and botanists call the high, or final, frontier.

As with every facet of this habitat, the statistics are phenomenal. One-third of the world's tropical woods – 2,500 tree species – occur only in the Amazon, some of them probably several hundred years old. Flowering plants (angiosperms) comprise about 90 per cent of the plant kingdom, and something in the region of 30,000 of them are known to science in Amazonia. Considering the canopy is so little explored, how many hundreds or thousands are still to be found and studied?

Flowers high in the forest canopy (clockwise from top left): **A parasitic plant related to the mistletoe; bromeliad; orchid; clusia flower**

Synergy in Action

Advertising is what it is really all about. When trees and plants are ready to have their flowers pollinated or their seeds dispersed, they must attract creatures that will do those vital tasks in the best possible way. When individual trees burst into flower the effect can be visually stunning, and locally the air maybe heavy with scent. None of this is of use, however, to those that don't have colour vision or a developed sense of smell; they have to be attracted in other ways. All trees and plants must offer some reward to those that visit, to make sure that they will always return. Nectar and nuts are just two of the prizes.

Many of the bits of the rainforest jigsaw started to fit together as I discovered more – particularly the crucial interdependency between animals and plants. The Brazil nut tree (*Bertholletia excelsa*) was just one perfect complicated example.

This giant of the forest depends for its existence on two very different creatures: one a bee, the other a rodent. The famous nuts are contained in a cannonball-shaped pod that weighs about 4.5 pounds (2 kg). There are usually between 15 and 25 nuts in each pod, and when they fall to the forest floor from 130 feet (40 metres) or more, they are potentially lethal to humans. Occasionally I would hear of someone being killed by one.

But before the tree can produce its seed crop, it has to first flower and persuade something to pollinate it. The Brazil nut's large, yellow flowers open during the day and are a complex arrangement that only one creature – the long-tongued orchid bee, or Euglossine – can negotiate. The flower contains a coiled, petal-like hood that closes tightly over itself. Only the orchid bee's strength and unusually long proboscis allow it to enter the flower and get at the nectar.

It seems that it's the larger female of the species that feeds on the flowers' nectar, during which process it transfers the pollen from one tree to another. The bees are strong fliers, which is just as well because Brazil nut trees grow widely apart. All attempts to cultivate plantations of Brazil nut trees have, until now, failed miserably. Orchid bees are non-social, solitary insects that will not congregate in traditional hives, and so they cannot be transported around man-made plantations. The tree, therefore, is dependent on this unique wild pollinator.

It takes up to fifteen months for the fruit pods to mature, after which they crash to the forest floor where the second crucial animal comes in to play. The pods are as hard as cement and only one creature in this rainforest can open them efficiently – the agouti. The agouti is a large rodent that looks like a cross between a rabbit and a tailless squirrel. It has front teeth as sharp as chisels, but even with these it can take as much as twenty minutes for it to open the pod.

The mature pods contain far more nuts than the agouti can eat at one sitting so, one by one, it takes away the remaining seeds, digs a hole and plants each nut before covering it up – at the perfect depth for it to germinate. After tamping the soil down on the nut, the agouti delicately places leaves over the spot to hide the evidence. It was wonderful to be able to watch this behaviour, hidden inside my filming hide and it always made me laugh because the agouti had no idea that someone knew where its secret hoard was buried. The agouti's poor memory is the tree's salvation: it simply cannot remember where it buries every nut and those that it forgets eventually germinate over twelve months later.

Opposite: **The tiny acouchi takes advantage of the Brazil nut pod opened by its larger relatives.** Above: **An Amazon squirrel investigates** *Dugetia* **fruit**

I eventually captured this behaviour on film from my hide, but getting a stills photograph was more problematic. The agouti is constantly alert to danger – it's a tasty meal for many predators here. My film camera was extremely quiet when it was running but just the sound of my rotting, fungus-covered still camera shutter being triggered would send the agouti fleeing as fast as a bullet. Having thrown away cameras and lenses every two years because of the humidity,

I decided to buy a completely new top-spec. Canon EOS 1V camera kit. The investment turned out to be very worthwhile.

I finally succeeded in getting the shots I wanted thanks to the camera's electronic wizardry. The problem was the light, or rather the lack of it. The few pictures I had taken were just too dark and, because of the agouti's nervous disposition, a flash was out of the question. So the simple answer, albeit an

expensive one, was to buy one of those wonderful image-stabilised zoom lenses.

I bought the 100–400mm zoom, and it was remarkable that I could rest the lens on the frame of my hide and, almost silently, rattle off dozens of shots that turned out sharp. Fancy being able to handhold a shot taken at one-thirtieth of a second and know that it will come out. I had never known such a thing. It amazed me.

The agouti, a vital rodent; if it were not for the agouti, the Brazil nut might well disappear

Brazil nuts are one of the most valuable crops for the local population. In 1970 the annual production was more than 100,000 tons; at present somewhere in the region of 40,000 tons are collected each year, mainly during the rain season. Local people gather almost all of these from wild rainforest trees. The benefits that native people receive from this annual harvest are thanks to the orchid bee and the agouti. If they disappear then, as sure as night follows day, so will the Brazil nut tree.

A bare-tailed woolly opossum, a nocturnal rodent that is active high in the trees at night

A Natural Stimulant

Commercially the rainforest is priceless, and I am not talking just of timber extraction. Apart from the inestimable wealth of medicinal plant potential, something humans have only just scratched the surface of, crops such as Brazil nuts, rubber, coffee, banana, pineapple, avocado, mango, paw paw, palm nuts and guarana are often the sole source of income for the people who live here.

The Satere Maues Indians first brought guarana to the attention of the outside world in the 1800s. The German naturalists Spix and Martius gave the plant its scientific name in 1820 when they travelled through the area. *Paullinia cupana* is a large climbing shrub whose striking-looking fruits produce an enormous annual cash crop. The harvest is so important to the country that a huge festival is held annually in Maues.

Historically, the Satere Maues Indians used a preparation of the leaves and roots of the plant to stun fish under water, but guarana also became famous as a treatment for many ailments, including headaches, fatigue and bowel complaints. It is still considered by many to be a potent aphrodisiac. Guarana has almost the same chemical composition as coffee, except that it contains three times the amount of caffeine. The annual harvest of about 2,500 tons is principally channelled to the home market where it is processed for beverages. However, it is becoming increasingly popular among some athletes and body builders, especially in the United States where it is called Zoom!

It was with the Satere that I first saw and tasted guarana. They had taken me to a forest-edge plantation where wild marmosets came to feed on the fruits. The marmosets only chew off the white pulp, letting the black seeds fall to the ground. My guide gave two of the seeds to me and told me to crush them in my mouth and then wash them down with a little water. The taste was extremely bitter and five minutes later my heart was palpitating.

Once the guarana seeds have been collected, they are washed, dry roasted and ground up. Sometimes when we were filming through the night, we would put a spoonful of the powder into a drink, which guaranteed that none of us would drop off at a crucial moment.

The Satere tell their children the legend of guarana. They say that Uniai, a Satere squaw, buried her child, which had been sired by a snake and killed by arrows fired by a monkey. After the child was buried, a plant grew from its eye sockets; and that's why the plant resembles human eyeballs.

What a charming bedtime story…

Guarana – for me, the most striking of all flowering plants.

A fruiting *Parkia* tree

A Sticky Solution

Besides the Brazil nut, I filmed two other very different fruiting strategies to illustrate the way in which trees attract specific pollinators and disperses. When the *Parkia pendula* tree is fruiting, it looks as though hundreds of bats are suspended from its branches. The 'bats' are, in fact, clusters of long, pendulous woody pods. These only open when the 20 to 30 seeds inside are mature. Normally when a pod opens, the seeds would simply fall to the forest floor and be eaten by rodents – but this tree has evolved the perfect solution to prevent that happening: glue.

The seeds are surrounded by a thick, gelatinous gum that holds them in place until creatures have had a chance to get at them. It is on this sticky gunge that the woolly monkey feeds. In the process of licking up the gum, however, the monkeys frequently swallow the seeds. A few hours later they pass them out a good distance away from the original tree – a perfect method of seed dispersal.

I had been told that another tiny primate regularly visited the tree when it contained fruit – the tiny pied bicolor tamarin. Like its close relative, the marmoset, the tamarin has a very small geographical distribution but my forest camp was, conveniently, in the centre of it. We had identified a massive *Parkia pendula* tree the previous year and built a bush ladder and filming platform into the 160-foot- (50-metre)-high crown, and as soon as the pods opened I virtually lived in the treetop for one week.

Almost every afternoon at about three o'clock, I would hear the unmistakeable high-pitched calls of a group of tamarins coming closer. They would group together in an adjacent tree that was shrouded in a creeping vine. Several pieces of this vine connected to the *Parkia* tree's lowest and longest branches, and the tamarins used this as a highway to get into the crown of the tree where they would run on all fours along the enormous *Parkia* limbs. Like high-wire circus performers, these miniature monkeys would then climb down the 3-foot- (1-metre)-long stalks to get at the fruit clusters, where they would hang by their hind legs and lick away at the gum for many minutes.

Above left: **An open *Parkia* fruit pod.** Above right: **A tamarin feeding on the gum**

Food of the Gods

The vast majority of trees produce flowers that open from buds that develop on new growth or leaf stems, but some produce them directly from the surface of the limbs or tree trunk itself. Botanists call this 'cauliflory', and of course our own vegetable cauliflower is a good example of something that grows directly on the stem of the plant.

The first cauliflorous tree that I discovered was *Theobroma cacao*, wild cacao, the original source of that wonderful confection, chocolate. (The word *theobroma* derives from the ancient Greek for 'Food of the Gods'.)

I watched and photographed a grey saki family come across the large green developing fruits that were growing straight off the trunk. Living in small family groups of an adult pair and their offspring, grey sakis are fabulous-looking monkeys with thick shaggy grey fur and short stubby tails – and are renowned for their spectacular leaping ability. They have relatively small home ranges of about 25 acres (10 hectares) but, as grey sakis prefer to live in the middle storey of the rainforest, they avoid competing with their larger relatives higher up in the crowns or with those creatures that eat mature seeds. I kept getting flashes of their dagger-like teeth as they ripped off the sweet fruit flesh to get at the young seeds inside. That's like you or I taking an apple, chewing and spitting out the flesh, and just swallowing the little black seeds in the centre.

In the interior of the forest, trees and foliage quickly absorb most sounds, but up in or above the canopy, carried by the air currents, it's a very different matter. Of natural sounds, birdcalls were the most commonly recognisable, then insects, but I would often hear quite distant groups of monkeys vocalising. Worryingly, the awful drone of the chainsaw could frequently be heard.

During my first few months of working in the canopy, one sound above all others intrigued me. It was a strange, growling, almost cat-like call and I was seriously frustrated at not knowing what it was. Then one day, I received a message from Peter Bassett, a producer with the BBC's Natural History Unit, who was working on David Attenborough's series, *The Life of Birds*. He asked me if I knew of the capuchin, or calf-bird. The mystery of the weird sound was about to be solved.

Above: **A wild cacao pod, 60 feet (20 metres) up and growing off the tree trunk.**
Right: **A grey saki, an essential destroyer of seeds**

CHAPTER 3

Wings of Mystery

"(Birds) are part of our world yet, at a clap of our hands, they lift into the air
and vanish into their own with a facility that we can only envy"

Sir David Attenborough
The Life of Birds (1998)

Nowhere else in the world do so many birds live. It's a simple but true statement. The continent of South America boasts 3,000 species, and Brazil alone is home to more than half of those. From tiny jewel-like hummingbirds to toucans that can justly be described as birds built to fly a beak, or the spectacular sight of the harpy eagle, the world's most powerful bird of prey, as a habitat the Amazon rainforest is without equal.

At dawn or dusk brilliant groups of macaws, parrots and oropendolas cross the rivers, leaving or returning to their traditional roost sites. During the day, roseate spoonbills, herons, storks, anhinga, kingfishers, skimmers, plovers and many other species are commonly sighted, and if you are interested in birds of prey then this place is paradise. Above the forest canopy or along the open rivers it is the spectacle of birds that impresses one, but in the deepest parts of the forest itself they often remain unseen. Their voices alone tease and frustrate us humans as we desperately try to find them.

An anhinga dries its wings after an underwater fishing session

The Mating Game

At just over 80 feet (25 metres) up, the tree is swaying about alarmingly. It's 5.15 a.m., I'm squeezed into a tiny canvas hide in which I cannot stand up or turn around, and I am getting cramps in my right leg. Everything, including my camera equipment, is soaking wet and I am dizzy from the constant swaying motion. I have been here for almost four weeks in an attempt to record one bird's bizarre mating ritual. It has never been filmed before – and I am beginning to understand why.

The Smithsonian Institute maintains an isolated forest reserve just over 40 miles (70 kilometres) north of Manaus. Twenty-five miles (40 kilometres) into the forest there is a small research station and it was here that I had come to try and find the calf-bird (*Perissocephalus tricolor*). I had spent five arduous days trekking through the forest, before dawn, with two expert Brazilian ornithologists. The terrain was severe in many parts with steep hills and uneven ground, but this was pristine rainforest and somewhere in here, my companions insisted, we would find male calf-birds.

They are one of the cotingas, a group of birds that incorporate spectacular displays when trying to attract a mate. The calf-bird's name comes from the bizarre sound that it makes, and on that first morning's hike, I heard the unmistakeable distant 'growl' that had baffled me for months around my own camp. '*Ave do Boi*', one of the birdmen said, the Portuguese name for the calf-bird. I almost couldn't believe it, as I had convinced myself it was some kind of arboreal cat. The strange call continued every half-minute and then others seemed to echo around it. At a guess

they were at least a third of a mile (half a kilometre) away.

It was hard going in the pre-dawn darkness and the forest floor had to be scanned carefully with torches for snakes. We had many encounters with venomous individuals here. By the time we arrived in the vicinity the calling had stopped. It was only six o'clock.

Enthusiastic birders always amaze me. Their talent for identifying a bird from the briefest glimpse and on many occasions just from an equally brief sound is an ability I sadly lack. One of my companions unclipped his backpack and produced a tape recorder. He pressed a button and the sound of a calf-bird calling played from the speaker. Seconds later, a loud reply came from a tree almost above our heads. Playback, as it is known, is a clever trick some ornithologists use to establish whether certain species are present, and it undoubtedly worked on this occasion. Looking through my binoculars I had my first-ever sighting of a male calf-bird. At first glance I thought it looked rather dull.

The following morning at five o'clock we were at the same spot. At nine minutes past, just as the first flecks of approaching daylight were touching the forest canopy, a drawn-out electronic-sounding moan echoed through the trees about us. Then it seemed that all hell was breaking out. It was one of the most incredible cacophonies that I had ever heard in the natural world. I could see the silhouettes of birds darting from branch to branch high above me, but most of the activity was hidden from view by foliage. My birdmen told me there were about twelve males and that this was their lek, a traditional site where male birds

A unique image from the lek – a male calf-bird in full display

display to impress the opposite sex. I knew that if I disturbed or frightened them they would move away and find another place. I was going to have to take great care and summon up every bit of patience I possessed.

Each dawn the show only lasted between ten and twenty minutes. The birds then moved further away to feed, but never too far from the lek or the females. Scaffolding was out of the question because of the distance to carry it, so I would have to build a wooden bush ladder up the side of the tree. The work would have to be done quickly, during the morning and early afternoon hours, before the birds returned at dusk.

After watching the display for three mornings I realised that the lek arena was quite well defined and that the birds kept to favourite branches. It's extremely difficult to judge from such an angle and distance, but after much indecision I picked the only tree that, from the ground, looked as if it would give me a clear view of the display. It seemed awfully close, only about 30 feet (10 metres) away, and the fork where I would build a small platform was more than 80 feet (25 metres) up.

It took four of us three days to carry the materials in, and two days to finish the ladder before putting my film hide in place. On a hot but breezy afternoon, I climbed up to test it and faced my first problem. The tree was swaying around in a 10–12 foot (3–4 metre) arc and it was a very unpleasant feeling. From the platform, however, the view was perfect. The surrounding trees formed a natural opening between my position and the display branches. The display branches themselves were easy to spot because for some reason they were noticeably bare of leaves.

I knew my only chance of getting shots of the calf-birds would mean having to climb the tree in the dark and without a torch. The birds roosted close to the lek at night, so it was vital that they did not see me climbing the tree. For the next two weeks I slogged almost 2 miles (3 kilometres) up hill, down valley, through creeks to the tree. At 3.30 a.m. with a safety harness around my waist, I edged my way up as quietly as possible, rung by rung, in total darkness to my hide. By the time I reached the top, I was sure the birds would hear my heart pounding in my chest.

My 300mm telephoto lens poked through the camouflage material of the film hide, and at ten minutes after five, the first bird called. Second problem: although my eyes could make out the birds, it was just too dark to film.

Frustration overwhelmed me as I watched the calf-birds, knowing that I was the first person ever to have such a privileged seat for their show. By half past five it was light enough to film, but the birds had stopped. I grabbed a few shots of them perched on branches preening themselves and then changed the lens on my camera. It made a tiny click as it came off – and there was a sudden flurry of wings outside. Looking through the small green mesh window of my hide I realised that all the birds had gone.

Perseverance and patience paid off two weeks later. One morning they must have slept in late because just before six, when I was thinking the worst, they all flew in and performed what I can only describe as a natural-history disco dance. The light was brilliant and those birds that I had first thought of as drab rocked and rolled in a dazzling display.

A male calf-bird. Of all the forest's sounds, the call of the calf-bird has to be the strangest

They have a naked blue face and forehead that seems to poke out from what looks like a hood of russet brown plumage. It's this monkish, cowl-like appearance that gives the bird its other name – the capuchin bird.

Males clearly have a dominant hierarchy among themselves. Display branches were defended vigorously with threatening body language and if that didn't work they would physically attack the upstart. Occasionally they would flap up and rip leaves off the branches, which is why the lek had a cleared or gardened look about it

As they puff themselves up ready to call, two beautiful bright orange feathers pop out from under their tails. The birds first lean forwards as they fill their throat sac with air, emitting a croak; then, raising themselves vertically erect, they let go a long meow sound; finally, leaning backwards as though they might fall off the branch, they let out a full roar. The whole effect is stunning and it is one of the weirdest sounds of the rainforest.

The males are competing with each other to attract the attention of a female. When she finally appears at the lek, the males go crazy. They call and posture almost without break and the noise is just about deafening. She sits quietly on a nearby branch watching and then, when she has made her choice, she will fly to his perch, peck him and allow him to mount her. It's all over in a few seconds. If only human courtship was that simple.

After almost four weeks, the daily trek in, the climb and then nine hours cramped in the hide, had left me feeling exhausted. But it was worth every minute of effort to finally capture the first-ever film of the calf birds' fascinating mating display.

A female calf-bird

Mutual Protection Racket

The single most important fact of life for many of the birds here is the loss of their eggs or young to predators. Many species camouflage their nests, or build them in a way that predators such as the kinkajou, snakes or arboreal carnivores will find it tricky to get at them. One group of birds has even discovered how to employ bodyguards – and I found that out the hard way.

During my first expeditions on the Rio Branco, in northern Brazil, I noticed tall emergent trees close to the edge of the river, with many strange sock-like structures hanging from their branches. These were 6½-feet (2-metre) long nests artfully woven by oropendolas, the idea being that they were putting them beyond the reach of predators. The birds were busy building the colony and their bright golden-yellow tails flashed among the open branches.

I wanted to get a panoramic shot of the river taken from up in the tree with those nests providing the foreground interest. We were carrying a couple of tons of metal scaffolding on our boat, so we tied up to the bank and set to work building an 80-foot (25-metre) tower.

We had become experts at erecting the metal towers and were up 30-feet (10-metres) in just three hours when work came to an abrupt stop. Three of us were trying to get down the scaffold corner poles as quickly as possible without falling, at the same time clutching at our heads and arms, which felt as if needles were being stabbed into them. We were under attack from venomous wasps. Crested oropendolas (*Psarocolius decumanus maculosus*) and some of their relatives regularly choose nest sites alongside those of wasps. Although I had read about this alliance in the past, I had

completely forgotten it. It was obvious that if we went any nearer the birds' nests, things would become unbearable. It seems that the wasps, too, benefit from this association. Some birds of prey and tamandua anteaters have been seen to regularly attack wasp nests, but if they venture close to an oropendola colony the birds will drive them off.

Using beekeepers' head nets, we dismantled the tower and moved it a good distance from the tree. Telephoto lenses had to be the answer until we had the correct protective clothing. We passed the afternoon watching and listening to the amazing courtship displays of the males. Clinging to the side of the suspended nests they would bow, and shake their wings so violently that they almost turned a full somersault. At the same time they produced the most fantastic musical bubbling sounds.

Months after the oropendola episode we were filming giant otters in a creek close to the Jauaperi River in northern Amazonia. Gordon, my assistant, and I were paddling our metal canoe when we rounded a bed and came across a superb sight.

The creek was only about 30 feet (10 metres) wide, with tall forest trees rising on both sides. A short distance from the muddy bank to our right, the top of a tree protruded from the dark still water. The branches had been colonised by yellow-rumped caciques, *Cacicus c. cela*, who were in the process of weaving twenty or more nests 3–6 feet (1–2 metres) above the water. The whole structure of interwoven nests seemed perilously close to the water surface.

A male cacique was perched on top of the mass of partly built nests. Its bright yellow beak and piercing blue eye followed us as we floated by. Without warning he started to ruffle his feathers fiercely, dipped his head and produced a shrill

sequence of rapidly ascending notes that reached a loud climax and ended suddenly. The effect of this call was to instantly bring several females out of the surrounding trees to the nests underneath him. It seemed as though he was encouraging them to get on with finishing the weaving work.

I thought that we might get an unusual shot of the cacique colony from under the water, so that afternoon I dived into the ever-sinister, dark creek. It was 40 feet (12 metres) to the bottom, where a terrific tangle of branches and forest debris had been snagged about the base of a tree trunk. At a depth of about 12 feet (4 metres), looking up, I could clearly see the colony of nests through the surface but something caught my attention in the murky water. I swam round to the far side of the tree where, suspended at an angle in the gentle current, were dozens of cacique nests. It was a surreal-looking sight. The birds had obviously been tragically caught out by unseasonably high rising water, and had rebuilt their colony at the very top of the tree, to avoid further disaster.

To get close-up sequences we moved the canoe very slowly towards the back of the colony. There I could see a branch sticking out, free of nests, which I thought Gordon could hold onto as I filmed. As we approached I put my hand out, and gently pulled on the branch. Something ricocheted off my forehead, then Gordon yelled loudly. Holding his eye with one hand, he paddled furiously backwards towards the far side of the creek. Careful inspection when things had calmed down revealed a brown paper-like structure the size of a watermelon in the middle of the nests. Caciques are very like oropendolas, just smaller, but for some reason my brain had not made the connection that afternoon.

Opposite: **A male, yellow-rumped cacique encouraging the females to weave their nests!**

"At first, the bird's confidence amazed us, and then it had us laughing. As David approached **the potoo** at the top of the tower, it went into full you-can't-see-me mode. Very slowly it stretched itself, pushing its tail feathers against the surface of the tree, where the connection was quite invisible, and then pointed its head skywards. To the uninitiated, it was a perfect stump of wood."

Mother of the Moon

There is something about hearing sounds that you cannot identify that intensifies the mystery of a wild place. In my first few months of living in the Amazon, it was a regular matter of recording sound tracks then playing them back to the locals in order to find out what was making a particular noise.

Once the sun had set, which it does quickly in equatorial regions, the combination of insects, frogs, rodents and nocturnal birds could be a surprisingly loud and constant chorus. Some first-time visitors to my camp found it impossible to

get to sleep until the small hours. Between midnight and four o'clock seemed to be the quietest time of the night but lying in my hammock, just occasionally, the roar of a male jaguar would raise the goose pimples on my neck or a shrill scream would punctuate the night as a predator took some creature. Life-and-death struggles continued round the clock here.

There is one sound that to me is more evocative of my years living in the forest than any other. It would be absent for weeks but, when the moon was almost full, for several nights the

Mother of the Moon – the nocturnal potoo, asleep but still able to see!

most mournful song would echo intermittently through the night – series of five or six descending melancholy notes that have prompted some to give the creature the onomatopoeic name, poor-me-all-alone. The locals call it Mother of the Moon and its one of the strangest birds in Amazonia. Its common name is the potoo, 'Nyctibius griseus'.

Only found in the hottest regions of South America, potoos are related to nightjars, but unlike nightjars they never perch on the ground. They have a wide, flat head containing large eyes and a huge mouth. The biggest of its kind can be a very impressive 3 feet (1 metre) tall. But it is this bird's ability to 'see with its eyes closed' that, perhaps, makes it most fascinating and this was the reason I accompanied David Attenborough on an expedition to film it.

For several days producer Peter Bassett, English ornithologist guide Andrew Whittaker and myself searched the trees bordering the creeks and narrower rivers on the south side of the Amazon close to a community called Manaquiri. I'd never seen a potoo in daylight. Andrew had explained that they were true experts at camouflage. So confident were they in their own invisibility, they would perch on open branches or tree stumps and would not take flight until you were just a few feet (a metre or so) away from them. Potoos have every right to consider themselves invisible – their plumage blends so perfectly with the tree bark that from just a short distance away they look exactly like a piece of the tree.

Andrew actually found two potoos on the third day's search. I would never have seen them, although now that I know what to look for I think I would stand a fair chance. The first one was in a tree that was unsuitable for filming, but the second potoo was only about 45 feet (14 metres) above the ground, almost on the edge of the river.

In order for me to film David next to the potoo, we had to build a scaffold tower. Despite our bird expert's opinion, I was convinced that hammering scaffolding together would frighten the potoo off to find a more peaceful sleeping place. Each step of the way I watched it closely.

Being so near to the bird, through my binoculars I could see what has been called the 'magic eye'. In daylight hours its eyes naturally close as it sleeps. I could clearly see two small notches in the upper eyelid, and it is through these that the bird can indeed see what is going on about it, without moving its head, even with its eyes closed.

At first, the bird's confidence amazed us, and then it had us laughing. As David approached the potoo at the top of the tower, it went into full you-can't-see-me mode. Very slowly it stretched itself, pushing its tail feathers against the surface of the tree, where the connection was quite invisible, and then pointed its head skywards. To the uninitiated, it looked just like a stump of wood. Its eyes were shut tight, but all the time it was watching David closely through its magic eye. The potoo wasn't in the least bit concerned by our presence; after all, it believed that we simply couldn't see it. It was wonderful to be able to observe such behaviour at close quarters.

The males of many species are fabulously coloured – this is an Andean cock of the rock

Above: **Sunbittern.** Above right: **A tropical screech owl feeding on a moth.** Right: **The bellbird has an amazingly loud call – like a hammer hitting a blacksmith's anvil**

There are few bird sightings in the rainforest to equal a flock of macaws, on the wing over the canopy – 'flying rainbows', my young daughter called them when she first saw them in the wild.

The splendour of a Jabiru stork on 6-foot (2-metre) wings gliding into the open crown of the most majestic of the Amazon's riverside trees, the samauma, always took my breath away. But fittingly for such an enigmatic ecosystem, some of the avian inhabitants have evolved astounding behaviour. I remember watching a leaf fall from a branch deep in the forest. It glided left and right on humid air, as all leaves do. But just before it touched the floor, it somehow changed and it took flight at such speed I was left wondering what on earth it was. It was, of course, a bird.

A hermit hummingbird – smaller than many of the flowers on which it feeds – in search of the nectar of *Inga* flowers

A blue and yellow macaw searching for seeds; macaws have excellent eyesight

In Brazil alone, 77 species of primates are known to science – by far the highest primate diversity of any country in the world. For anyone who is besotted by monkeys, it is the place to be. On the ground, staggering about in the undergrowth, tripping over tree roots, developing a pain in the neck from hours of gazing upwards, all we can usually see of our relatives are brief glimpses of branch movements and the occasional silhouette as one leaps from a branch. Their kingdom is some 100 feet (30 metres) or more above the ground and if we want to observe them closely there is only one solution: to be up there with them. That means building 150-foot (46-metre) towers into the roof of the forest – and this is the habitat we explore in the next chapter.

The dazzling coloured feathers of macaws are sought after by many forest-dwelling people for use as decoration

The toucan uses its huge beak with incredible dexterity to extract fruits; toucans are vital seed dispersers in the rainforest

CHAPTER 4

Web of the Spider Monkey

"... There was something human-like in its appearance, as the lean, dark, shaggy creature moved deliberately amongst the branches at a great height..."

Henry Walter Bates
The Naturalist on the Amazons (1864)

In 1992, a ship set sail from London docks carrying 12 tons of German-designed scaffolding. Labels on the crates grandly announced that the final destination address was: Nick Gordon, Alligator Creek, The Amazon. There was no postal or zip code, of course, and its actual drop-off point was the port of Manaus in the heart of the Amazonia. For my team and me this was just the beginning. We had to transfer the tons of metal by boat, then small canoe, to my remote camp in the forest.

Three months later we had the first of six towers in place. Noise and human disturbance from constructing the tower had sent most living creatures scurrying from the immediate area, but I knew it would only be a matter of a few weeks before they came back. There was a tree crammed with fruit that some monkeys would not be able to resist. In the meantime, I contented myself with the spectacular views of the rainforest canopy.

Being on top of the tower at any time, but especially at dawn or dusk, was the perfect cure for claustrophobic feelings. Months of exploring the forest floor had taken their toll on me. In time I would spend many nights sleeping up there, the only way to be certain of avoiding being seen by the monkeys. Those nocturnal experiences were unique. How many people ever get to sleep on top of the greatest forest on our planet? And, oh, the stars!

I had been commissioned to make two films about primates. The first one was to concentrate on one of the largest monkeys, *Ateles paniscus*, the black spider monkey. Others that we were to include in the film, such as the woolly monkey or the howler may come close in body weight, but they could never compare with the spider monkey's agility.

For the first few months I did wonder at times if I would ever complete the film. Day after day, week after week, we would trek for miles through the pristine forest, returning to camp at dusk exhausted and disheartened having seen nothing of them. Eventually our patience paid off.

Opposite: **Spider monkeys hanging from a canopy branch at dawn**

It was 4.40 a.m., dawn was an hour away. The evening before, I had watched a family of spider monkeys settle in the treetop for the night, the first time a group had come close enough to my camera tower to film at daybreak. All I had to do now – after surviving the terrifying and backbreaking process of climbing the 150-foot (46-metre) tower in the pitch dark – was wait.

Just before 6 a.m., toucans began calling and macaws started squabbling – a sure sign that the day was beginning. I wiped the condensation off the camera's viewfinder and looked through. Just over 20 feet (7 metres) in front of me, a large huddle of black fur began to untangle itself as the six spider monkeys began slowly waking up. They scratched, yawned, and stretched lazily. Three of them groomed each other's long, black, hairy bodies, and two adults loped away to the end of a branch.

As the sun drenched the rainforest canopy in a deep gold, the monkeys used their long arms and prehensile tails to hang off the branch – they were sunbathing! Looking at them this way, it was clear why these primates had been given their name: with their limbs spread, silhouetted against the deep blue sky, they looked incredibly spider-like. I spent two years observing spider monkeys, but it is always this image of them sunbathing on that first filming morning that comes to mind when I think of my time with them.

I first saw spider monkeys in the wild on 14 May 1993, a year after coming to Brazilian Amazonia. It was a baking hot afternoon, and my assistant and I had been following a group of giant otters for hours. We were relaxing at the edge of a creek when we heard a commotion in the treetops behind us. There, more than 100 feet (30 metres) up, seven large, black monkeys were clearly having a great time. The tree they were in was laden with tangerine-sized, bright yellow fruits. They chuckled and screamed for half an hour as they stuffed themselves with the fruit, before slumping into what seemed like torpor.

Back at our base, a 70-tonne riverboat on the Rio Branco five days' sail north of Manaus, we met a botanist who had come to explore the area. I told him about the spider-monkey behaviour I had seen that afternoon. He had studied black spider monkeys for four years and was a mine of information. He told me that the group we had watched that afternoon had been getting drunk on fermenting fruits. As I imagined capturing that scene on film, the seeds of a future project were sown.

Above left: **A black-faced male spider monkey.** Above: **A woolly monkey has a similar body weight, but cannot match the spider monkey's agility**

Above: A red-faced spider monkey getting drunk on fermenting fruit

A female spider monkey yawns as she wakes up; the forest canopy and sunrise are reflected in her eyes

The rainforest's complexity is difficult enough to explain in simple words, but film is a completely different matter. What I had wanted to do for several years was achieve a simple, entertaining story showing how it all fitted together. After meeting with several botanists, I could see how the spider monkey would tell that story perfectly. It specialises in eating the fruits of many big forest trees, and because it swallows fruit without chewing, the seeds are eventually passed out, usually far from the tree where they were picked – the parent tree, as we call it. This is the perfect seed-dispersal strategy, and the very reason those spider monkeys – and some of their relatives – are so vital in the order of things.

Unfortunately for the spider monkey, though, those same big trees are also valuable to us humans as timber – and here lies conflict. When the trees are removed by logging, the spider monkey loses a primary source of food and has to move away from the area. But the other side of the coin is equally important: if the spider monkey is removed by over-hunting (a danger in many areas), then the tree's seeds will no longer be dispersed and the trees will surely disappear. It's a very simple concept, but many humans seem unable to take it on – because, I think, the timescale of a rainforest tree's life is so much longer than our own.

Right: **A juvenile nibbles a branch to get at the sap**

"Watching spider monkeys play **is a delight.** A youngster will watch an adult's tail, **suddenly bite it** and run away. In return, the adults sometimes **chastise the young with a slap.**"

Our treetop family was, I had been told, a typical spider monkey group, though some may number as many as nine or as few as four. I was watching three females, one with a baby male about four months old, and two males.

The females rule spider monkey society. The group's dominant female leads them about their territory throughout the year, and she will choose a male when she is ready to mate. Each group has a maximum home range of almost 2,500 acres (roughly 1,000 hectares), which they know intimately. A good memory for the available food sources is essential during the long five months when fruits are scarce. I witnessed the perfect example of this one October. It was two months before the rains were due – famine time for many creatures here, including the spider monkeys. They had to range further afield each day to find food.

The dominant female led the family, and I followed them for about half a mile (one kilometre) without stopping once. Clearly she knew where she was heading. Spider monkeys can travel with exceptional speed through the treetops – much faster than us humans on the ground far below.

They settled in a middle-storey Naucleopsis tree. There were only about two dozen spiky, tennis ball-sized fruits, most still green, among the spindly branches. A few yellow fruits were greedily gorged on. Then the monkeys gently nibbled some of the green fruits until a thick, white liquid dripped from the spikes. They actually returned to that same tree one week later and polished off the remaining fruits that had turned yellow and were ready to eat. One botanist told me that he thought the nibbling of the green fruit helped to provoke faster maturity. That seems like very intelligent monkey behaviour to me.

Red-faced spider monkeys

Whatever the month, feast or famine, spider-monkey activity is usually the same. After a slow wake-up, they feed for up to an hour and a half. After this, rest and play take over for two hours, followed by another feeding session. During the hottest hours, they drape themselves over high canopy branches to make the most of any available breeze. Sometimes, they turn their faces into the wind and stick out their small pink tongues – another cooling-down strategy, presumably. After cooling-off, there is a final afternoon bout of feeding and socialising.

Watching spider monkeys play is a delight. A youngster will watch an adult's tail, suddenly bite it and run away. In return, the adults sometimes chastise the young with a slap. On occasions, all of them play a kind of tag in which they chase an individual until it is caught, then it runs off after the others in hot pursuit until it manages a grab or a playful bite.

And so it goes on. Once, I was filming an adult hanging from a lofty branch by her tail. Another monkey came along and bit her tail to make her drop off the branch, which she did. But then roles were reversed and she did the same to her antagonist. It was hilarious to observe.

The spider monkey has longer limbs than any other primate in Amazonia. Its tail is an effective fifth limb that can grasp with surprising strength. It often uses it to hang from a branch so that its hands are free to get at fruit beyond normal reach. It moves from tree to tree with exceptional speed, by brachiating – swinging arm over arm – with fluid grace and timing. As young spider monkeys start to move about alone (a risky time), the tail is used in a special way. When the next tree is a bit too far for an infant to leap to, an adult female (I never saw a male do this) holds one branch with her hands and the other with her tail, spanning gaps as much as 10 feet (3 metres) wide. The infant then scrabbles across this 'furry bridge', holding on to the adult's long hair.

When the rains start, the monkeys spend their time sheltering as best they can. Their thick, black, shaggy coat seems to shed rain well, unless a deluge goes on all day. In this case, they huddle together, except for the guard male who is usually some distance away with a good view of the vicinity. Fortunately, the rain season coincides with an abundance of fruit, so at least they don't have to travel so far to feed. At this time, their home ranges are considerably smaller. In my experience, only two factors alter the monkey's normal pattern of behaviour: heavy rain or the presence of a predator.

Above: **Prehensile (grasping) tails allow the monkeys to get at fruits that would otherwise be out of hands' reach**

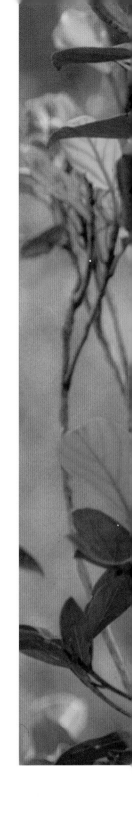

Once, I was watching a group feeding in one of the highest emergent trees when a great commotion suddenly started. They were alarm calling, an amazing thing to both hear and see. The guard male had clearly seen something and was cough-calling, as I called it, swinging backwards and forwards on his branch with his eyes fixed on another tree. The rest of the group was looking in the same direction, shaking the branches with their arms and legs, their faces displaying real anger. Their long, grasping tails were securely anchored to the branches above. The dominant female was echoing the guard male's shouts in a duet. The rest screamed and called, too – so loudly that I wondered how they avoided sore throats.

It took me some time to find the cause of this alarm. Then, from the other side of my filming hide, I saw a harpy eagle perched in a nearby tree with a clear view of the monkeys. Its magnificent head bobbed about in a circular movement as it sized up the distance to a possible meal.

Apart from humans, this bird must be the biggest danger the monkeys face. After ten minutes, the eagle realised it had been detected and flew off in search of other prey. But the monkeys didn't stop alarm calling for another half hour. Even then, they kept close watch on the now empty tree.

Forest people regard monkeys, especially large ones, as prize food. Where there are shotguns, monkeys of any kind are hard to find, having long moved away or become locally extinct. Where Indians still hunt with traditional weapons, such as blowpipes, monkeys exist in seemingly healthy numbers, at least where I have travelled. I often have to remind myself that the people need to hunt and, I like to believe, have little serious impact on the forest population of monkeys. Nevertheless, when I saw some Matis Indians return from a four-day hunt carrying the bodies of five adult spider monkeys, I shuddered at the thought of the family left in tatters.

In the end, I came to know spider monkeys in a way I could never have imagined. One day, an eight-week-old male was plonked into my arms. His tiny, emaciated body weighed just over half a pound (less than 0.5kg). He seemed doomed to die, having survived a fall, clinging to his mother as she fell, shot dead from a treetop. He held tight to me, making a feeble 'peet-peet' sound, and I knew I couldn't abandon him. I named him Pete and took him to my forest camp.

A month later, he had recovered his health, grown a little and lived free in the forest around my hut. Our lives were never the same after Pete arrived. He filled our days with unimaginable pleasure and fun, though at times he could be an infuriating menace. He accompanied me everywhere, usually on my shoulders, as I paddled up creeks in my canoe, walked through the forest or climbed my filming towers. There, he would wait patiently on top, looking scornfully down at me as I struggled up. He helped me in many ways too. He always found

With Pete, my pet spider monkey. He coulld climb to the top of my filming towers far more quickly than I could!

"Our lives were never the same after Pete arrived. He filled our days with **unimaginable** pleasure and fun, though at times he could be an infuriating menace. He accompanied me everywhere – I think he even saved my life one day."

fruiting trees or other groups of monkeys where I would never have done.

I think he even saved my life one day. Late one afternoon, while walking a forest trail back to camp, Pete was, as usual, enjoying a free shoulder ride, his hands gripping my hair. Then, without warning, he leapt off and attacked something on the ground just a few metres in front of us. It was a potentially lethal fer-de-lance snake, and I have no doubt that I would have either stepped on it or close enough to it for it to strike. Pete had spotted it, despite the snake's cryptic colouring. I screamed at him to get away as the snake struck at him twice.

This showed me what exceptional vision spider monkeys have. I also came to know spider monkey vocalisations through Pete. I could tell from his voice when he was happy, sad, scared or angry. And I came to recognise what was happening in a wild group because they made the same sounds.

I only wish Pete's story had a happy ending. He disappeared one afternoon when he was four years old and I never saw him alive again. We eventually discovered, after four weeks' of desperate searching, that a hunter had shot him. With that news, one of the happiest periods of my life in the rainforest came to an end. Even now, five years later, I miss his company. I especially remember how, when I was in my hammock sick with malaria, he would sit on my legs, eyes downcast, suffering along with me. At least I have the small consolation of knowing that he enjoyed four good years of life with us.

Without doubt, my most memorable observation of wild spider monkeys came almost at the end of my project. It was at the Smithsonian Institute's forest reserve, about 40 miles (70 kilometres) northwest of Manaus, where I was filming calf-birds for David Attenborough's series *The Life of Birds*. Each day for a month as I trudged along the trails to my tree tower, I would

see a group of eight spider monkeys, and I could tell precisely what they were up to. The tree they were in was crammed with overripe and fermenting orange-coloured fruits, and they were stuffing themselves with them – getting drunk. Their play was much more boisterous than usual: one adult threw a mushy fruit at another that was chasing him. It missed. They licked their sticky fingers and their faces became caked with the fruit pulp, like toddlers at a tea party. One of them leapt out to catch a nearby branch and fell more than 65 feet (20 metres) to a lower limb. Unshaken, he ran back up to continue the affray.

I watched this enchanting scene for an hour, by which time the monkeys were either draped over boughs or wedged into the forks of branches, heads drooped, hands and feet hanging, tails looped around branches. It wasn't hard to imagine how they would feel the morning after. For me, it was the perfect afternoon – almost. I only wish Pete could have been there too.

Gremlins of the Forest

Spider and woolly monkeys are two of the heavyweights in the forest, but Amazonia is also home to the smallest monkeys in the world and my next film project was to focus closely on their natural history.

Marmosets and tamarins are a fascinating group. To date, eighteen species of marmoset are known to science, seventeen of which are endemic to Brazil. There are twelve species of tamarin, including the lion tamarins from the devastated Atlantic forest in the south of Brazil. They differ from marmosets principally because of their dentition. Unlike the marmosets, tamarins do not have the chisel-like front lower teeth that they use to gouge wood, allowing them to feed on the gums and saps that trees produce. This is a vital source of food when fruit is scarce.

We were working almost 200 miles (320 kilometres) southeast of my home camp, south of the Amazon River. This region is home to the Satere Maues Indians, who believe that the tiny marmosets are reincarnations of their dead children. Our year and a half filming them, and the monkeys, immersed us in yet another intriguing Amerindian culture and was, eventually, to lead us to a unique discovery.

A glance at the map of marmoset population distribution south of the Amazon immediately highlights one fact. These tiny monkeys cannot swim, so crossing the rivers to increase territory is not possible. They have, therefore, become isolated in forest areas between major watercourses. It is because of this that they have evolved their many different physical appearances. They have long, non-prehensile tails and their heads are variously decorated with tufts, tassels, manes, ruffs, moustaches and mantles of long hair.

Small enough to fit comfortably in a human hand, they clearly resemble Spielberg's infamous creatures in his film, *Gremlins*. Having watched them at close quarters for some years, I can confirm that they do in fact share some of their fictional relative's characteristics, too.

Twin marmosets at six weeks of age: they will soon be too heavy for their father to carry

"Small enough to fit comfortably in a human hand,

they clearly resemble Spielberg's

infamous creatures in his film, *Gremlins.*

Having watched them at close quarters for some years,

I can confirm that they **do in fact** share some of their

fictional relative's **characteristics.**"

For the first 14 months, I concentrated on the striking golden white tassel-eared marmoset, *Mico chrysoleucus*, closely following one tight-knit family of seven individuals. They live in the middle to lower layer of the forest canopy but, unusually for monkeys, quite frequently visit the ground. In behavioural terms they are completely absorbing. The family is extremely social, constantly keeping in contact with each other using high-pitched, almost bird-like, calls. Many pairs of eyes, of course, also improve the chances of spotting danger, and in this forest there's plenty to watch out for. Being so small they are vulnerable to predation by birds of prey, snakes and small cats, but fortunately for these monkeys, they are so small as to not be sought after as food by man.

A marmoset's average weight is between 12 and 14 ounces (350 and 400 grams) and the females are generally slightly heavier than the males. They can walk and run on all fours along branches and cling vertically to the sides of trees. Despite their diminutive size, they can leap exceptionally well, frequently jumping gaps of 13–16 feet (4–5 metres). They can also hang from a branch by their hind limbs. Although they feed primarily on insects, fruit, saps and gums, they will also prey on small birds or their eggs, frogs, lizards, snails and even small snakes.

There is one aspect of their natural history that sets them apart from other primates. Rather than the mother caring solely for her offspring, in marmoset society all members of the group cooperate in the rearing of the young, especially the males. I witnessed this from a very privileged position one night.

I had watched the family throughout the day, convinced that the dominant female was very close to giving birth. She was clearly heavily pregnant and in the previous few days had been having a little trouble in getting about. Marmosets are diurnal and pass the nights in tree holes or thick tangles of vines, almost never using the same place on consecutive nights. One of the reasons for such vigilance, it is thought, is that during the night they experience a form of torpor similar to that seen in many small hibernating mammals. Their metabolic rate is greatly reduced when their body temperature drops as much as 6°F (about 4°C). In this condition they are much less alert to danger and they would be unable, in many cases, to escape a predator.

Opposite: **A golden white tassel-eared marmoset feeding on guarana fruits.** Above: **New-born twin marmosets cling tightly to their father**

On this particular afternoon, my group had come close to a tree hole almost an hour earlier than they would normally do. I had already cut away a filming window through the back of the thick trunk and covered it with camouflaged material. My camera had been in position there for several days to avoid disturbance. This was the fifth time I had set up my camera in tree holes and I was very aware that no one had ever filmed a marmoset birth before. I frequently wondered whether my perseverance would ever pay off.

It was 5.40 p.m., the blistering afternoon heat finally abating. The family were silent so close to their chosen overnight sleeping place; they didn't want to alert any potential predators to their whereabouts – especially tonight. Instead of calling to one another they followed their strong-smelling scent trails, frequently stopping and scanning the ground for danger. Through a slit in my hide, I watched as the female made her way slowly from several trees away. She obviously couldn't leap any more and was using the connecting vegetation of palm leaves to travel between the trees. She entered the hole first and sniffed, carefully, the small den floor. I held my breath, praying that she would not smell me.

After about 30 seconds she leaned against the wall, her tummy so swollen it was obviously making her extremely uncomfortable. Minutes later, the rest of the group came in and all huddled up against her. Many times over the next two hours some of them would break away from the furry scrum and peer into the camera lens, tilting their heads from side to side in curiosity. I am sure that it was their own reflection that intrigued them, but it took all my self-control not to laugh out loud as they peered down my lens.

By eight o'clock they were all settled, camera lens forgotten and deep in sleep – except for the female. She simply couldn't relax. Despite the fact that I was sitting there doing little but peer through a camera viewfinder, it was mentally draining. Occasionally I would bring my eye away and quietly wipe the sweat and mosquitoes off with a towel. As I put my eye back to the viewfinder I thought I saw something happen. Had she pulled a face as though she were in great pain? I wondered if I had imagined it – then she did it again. Her face contorted and she shifted her position away from the others, holding on to the rough wood forming the inside of the hole. She was in labour.

It was tremendous being so close to them, just a foot (30 centimetres) in front of my lens and totally unaware of my presence. I could actually smell them and hear her little whimpers of pain, but I still hadn't totally convinced myself, and I actually wondered at one point if she might have food poisoning! The grimacing with each contraction reminded me of the many times I had suffered abdominal cramps. Her spasms came every four minutes for the first half an hour, after which she contracted once every minute until the first tiny head appeared.

Sitting upright, she delivered the baby herself by cradling its head and gently pulling. Then, bending forwards, she started to lick him clean until the rest of him slipped out and he immediately found her breast. He was no bigger than my thumb. There were no cries, which could attract attention to the hole, just barely audible trills, and at this stage the dominant male was oblivious to the proceedings – fast asleep.

She started to contract again almost immediately and five minutes later a second baby was born just inches from my face – a truly moving experience. These monkeys usually give birth to twins and at birth they represent 20 per cent of the female's body weight. To give that statistic a comparison, it is the equivalent of a human mother giving birth to a 30-pound (13.5-kilogram) baby. The thought made my eyes water.

The male, now awake, turned his attention to the placenta and, after eating this, he chewed off the umbilical cords. The female, exhausted, slept soundly as the male licked each infant's face in turn taking them off their mother and on to his own chest. From now on, the only contact the female would have with her infants would be to suckle them.

We followed the infants' development over the next twelve weeks. Observing and filming them as they took their own first independent steps away from the adults' backs, and coming face to face with some of their forest's dangers – like the venomous centipede *Scolopendra* – was, for us, a once-in-a-lifetime experience. Between eight and ten weeks old the infants are fully weaned and then, for the most part, have to get their own food – or steal it from the adults.

Once the golden white tassel-eared marmoset has removed the giant grub's pincers, it can be eaten safely

Discovery of a Lifetime

Although we had captured the first ever birth of marmosets on film, the greatest prize was yet to come.

Our early expeditions to the Satere territory had revealed a puzzle that we were anxious to solve. Some of the villagers at Bom Futura had looked at our pictures of the three species that we knew existed in the area and had told us, confidently, many times that they knew of another very different marmoset. Over many years living in the Amazon forest I had come to realise that one had to be extremely circumspect about such claims. Many of the local inhabitants have fantastic tales of creatures that simply do not exist outside their imaginations and folklore.

They were telling us of a tiny monkey (*macaquinho* in Portuguese) that had naked ears, and this certainly was unknown to us, and to the primate experts that we talked to. We decided to mount an expedition specifically to investigate the story, to the area where they told us it could be found. Even more remarkable was that they told us they knew of a Satere community in which the people kept one or two as pets.

After three days' sailing east down the Amazon River, we turned south into the wonderfully named Pineapple River. Our fixer,

Valquimar, suggested that he went ahead in the fast canoe, to get permission for our visit from the chief of the community, an essential protocol we had learned. I could never have imagined what tale he would return with the next day.

We already knew that forest people occasionally kept marmosets as pets. Some of the women wear them in their hair through the day where they happily perch, cleaning the scalp of *piolhos* – nits! I didn't believe for one minute that we were going to find a species, new to science, munching lice on a Satere woman's head.

Valquimar returned at dawn the next day with the welcome news that we had the Chief's permission to stay with the Satere and, even better, that they were preparing for their annual ritual, the Dance of the Tocandeiro. I had heard of this rite before. Young Satere boys suffer the most painful initiation ceremony imaginable to us outsiders. Hundreds of enormous venomous ants are collected from their nests and woven into a palm glove. Each young initiate has to put his hands into the glove for a few minutes while dancing. The Satere believe that surviving this ceremony proves strength and builds resistance to dangers within their forest. I think it also impresses the girls.

Above: **There is something almost human in the Satere marmoset's facial expression.** Opposite: **The Satere marmoset**

The ant "glove" used in the Satere Indians' initiation ceremony

The Tocandeiro ants are collected at dawn and we were invited along to film the event. I already knew these ants by a different name. To us they were 24-Hour Ants because if you were stung by one it took that long for the excruciating pain to go away. I had never seen their nests, though.

The men were searching around the bases of trees. The entrance to the nest is a series of smooth-edged holes, quite distinctive. One man has a 3-foot (1-metre) thin stick that he taps against the chosen tree, just above the holes. Within seconds, a dozen or more 2-inch (5-cm) ants were scrabbling out to attack the intruder. Not only do they have the painful venomous sting in their tail, they also have formidable biting mandibles. The stick was then offered to each ant, which instinctively grabbed it with its jaws. One by one, more than 200 were then tapped off into a long bamboo tube made especially to store the ants.

Back across the river, the party was in full swing. Some leaves had been collected from a cashew nut tree, packed with the delicious mature fruits, and these were crushed by hand and mixed into a large bowl of river water. The ants were then literally poured into the liquid. Within seconds they appeared to be quite dead.

Two men sat on a log and inserted the ants, one at a time, into the weave of a glove made from palm fronds. All of them had their stings pointing in towards the inside of the glove. It took about 45 minutes, by which time the ants were coming back to life bristling with anger. I simply couldn't come to terms with the thought that anybody was going to stick their hand in it – but that is exactly what they did.

"Two men sat on a log and inserted the ants, one at a time, into the weave of a glove made from palm fronds. All of them had their stings pointing in towards the inside of the glove. It took about 45 minutes, by which time the ants were coming back to life bristling with anger. I simply couldn't come to terms with the thought that anybody was going to stick their hand in it – but that is exactly what they did."

Under the thatched canopy of an open-sided hut, a line of ten men chanted and danced forwards and backwards, securing the initiate by his arms. Another man stepped forward with the glove, now decorated with margay cat skin and macaw feathers, and held it out. The line of dancers came forward and a young boy, just 12 years old, lifted his right arm. As his hand entered the glove, his head dropped and he began to weep with pain.

This ceremonial party went on throughout the night although we left them to it just after midnight. The following morning I was anxious to find the young boy and see how he was. We found him behind a hut kicking a ball about with some friends, seemingly none the worse for his ordeal. A group of girls were watching him, clearly impressed.

The village chief had given Valquimar instructions on how to find the community with the unknown marmoset. By the following morning we had found the place some 10 miles (16 kilometres) further up the river and met the family who confirmed that they had one of the marmosets we were looking for. At the river edge a young girl stepped out of a canoe and came towards us: on her head was a completely new species of marmoset. We were enthralled.

This tiny monkey was indeed different to any others of its kind that I had seen because it had naked ears. Like all the other marmosets it had claws instead of nails, a long, non-prehensile tail, and teeth that could gouge holes in tree trunks – and my fingers! The girl's father said he could take us into the forest where he could show us the wild group that this baby had been taken from.

Two hours later we were hearing the classic, cryptic bird-like calls of the family, and minutes later I was filming them. Scientists have named it *Mico saterei* after the Satere people who have, of course, always known of the monkey's existence. I took a photograph of one that I still regard as one of the most special images I have captured in all my years in this rainforest.

Above: 'Face-pulling,' a common way of communicating between marmosets

Above: A moustached tamarin 'tongue flicking' – a facial display that says 'keep away from me.' Above right: A satere checking out the camera!

CHAPTER 5

The Secret Earth

"... For the mind sees this forest better than the eye. The mind is not deceived by what merely shows"

Henry Major Tomlinson
The Sea and the Jungle (1912)

Less than one per cent of the daylight that bathes the canopy reaches the forest floor. It is gloomy, very quiet and eerily still most of the time. As you walk, your feet sink into ankle-deep, soft rotting vegetation. Ants rummage everywhere and alien-like fungus forms cover dying leaves and old fallen trees. Yet the dark forest floor is a paradox because, despite the lack of light, this is where most plant life must begin. One way or another, everything must grow upon it.

At first, the odds seem stacked against anything surviving here. Rainforest soils, despite appearances, are famously nutrient poor and shallow. The thin soil layer is covered by a couple of inches (6 centimetres) of humus created by millions of dead leaves that fall from above. Decomposing ants, termites, and animals join bacteria and fungus hard at work breaking everything down.

One of the first things that took my breath away was the size of the trees. Generally, they are huge. The irony of this situation is visible to my eye. Enormous buttresses support many of those that tower above me. Some of them snake out far across the floor. Many others are held upright by dozens of umbrella-like roots – but these roots are several yards (3 metres) above the ground, and I can walk under them. Others are covered in razor-sharp thorns to protect them. Without these support systems above ground, the trees would simply fall over.

After a while you start to notice things. Something tiny scurries from one leaf to the cover of another. What was that? Leaves and shreds of dead wood move, but not because of any breeze. There is another hidden world here, and it is literally crawling with life. It is here to discover for those who know where, or how, to look – and it is vital to pay attention to where you are stepping! Apart from countless thorns and spines that can rip clothing and flesh in an alarmingly effortless fashion, there are invisible holes excavated by animals or where trees once stood, that can easily break a human leg.

It is a fact that most creatures down here do not want to draw attention to themselves, so they have evolved camouflage, cryptic patterns or colours to blend perfectly with their surroundings. This is a good survival strategy and, whether you are the one doing the hunting or the one being hunted, not being seen can be crucial.

Opposite: Fungus cups sprouting from a fallen decaying tree trunk. Above: Even before a dead tree falls, fungi emerge to consume it

Survival Strategies

It was immediately apparent how, with a little detective work, the forest floor could tell me what was going on out of sight in the canopy more than 130 feet (40 metres) above me.

Fallen fruits, partly eaten, usually meant there were monkeys about. Fruits peeled open, with the seeds gone, told me that flocks of parrots had passed by. Thousands of ants scurry across the floor, up and down the side of a tree trunk, many carrying small, white maggot-like larvae. They are army ants, robbing a wasps' nest in the highest branches. I break open small, dark, moist pellets – monkey droppings – and see small seeds. I know that in one week the seeds can start to germinate and I could find a shoot growing. Then the battle to survive really starts.

Many creatures love the juicy new growth of seedlings – rodents, birds, wild pigs, tapirs, deer and others constantly browse the forest floor. It is not easy to make a living in the Amazon rainforest, and whether you are a tree, plant or animal, finding enough food is a constant struggle. This is why it is so difficult to see most of the creatures that live here. I also noticed that trees of the same type were often separated by hundreds of metres and sometimes kilometres. That is why there can be two hundred different species of tree in just 2.5 acres (1 hectare) – that is biodiversity.

But the trees' strategies are 'intelligent'. They have evolved over hundreds of thousands of years and, as crazy as it sounds, there were times when I did wonder whether trees could somehow think!

An individual tree can produce a large crop of seeds, most of which will be destroyed. But their very destruction is vital here. Those seeds are eaten, providing, at times, the only food available for many creatures. And this is the pay-off. For the tree to be successful – in other words, to guarantee the future of its own species – it must make sure that another is there to replace it when it finally dies and falls. So, in very simple terms, it needs only one of its seeds to make it to maturity.

Opposite: **Rainwater collects in huge woody fungus bowls.**
Above: **Caterpillars herd together for safety from predators**

Fatal Attraction

Every minute of every day, life-and-death dramas are being played out. It is the way of things here. I remember the first time I focused my camera on a place where many fruits had fallen. I had built a camera hide so that I would be invisible to any visitors. Within one hour some birds had arrived. The first surprise for me was to see a toucan land on the ground and throw several seeds back into its massive, gaping beak. I had always thought that toucans only fed up in the trees. After the toucans a yellow foot tortoise shuffled slowly about, mashing the fruit pulp away from the hard seed. By now, ants, wasps and butterflies were all over the sticky fruits. And that was just the day shift.

At night an entirely different community is at large and Amazonia is anything but quiet. As the last rays of daylight fade, everything under the forest canopy is plunged into darkness. A symphony of insects, frogs and nocturnal animals call – living audible proof of the diversity here. On my first two nights in the hide, I filmed a paca that had come in to eat the fruits. These huge rodents don't just eat the fruits' flesh – they chew the seeds up too. On occasions, that can prove to be fatal.

Among the animals, plants and trees, competition to survive is fierce. Many of them protect themselves from potential predators in clever ways. Spines and thorns are easily seen and felt – but there are some plants that use toxins and poisons to make themselves unpalatable. During the making of my spider monkey film, I filmed the monkeys eating fruit from a *Strychnos* vine. It is where strychnine was discovered in the first place. This large vine droops from the highest trees all the way down to the forest floor. When its seeds are mature it relies on animals to disperse them so it surrounds the seed with a sweet irresistible pulp – but that seed is laced with the deadly poison.

Spider monkeys swallow fruits whole and it's their digestive system that removes the fruit flesh from the seed. The seed, of course, is then passed out, but the spider monkey is unharmed. Pacas, clearly, are not as intelligent as spider monkeys. Once, at the base of a *Strychnos* vine, I found a dead paca. All about its body were fallen fruits from the vine. The paca chews the fruit and seed before swallowing. I suspect that pacas and other rodents know instinctively that such fruits should be avoided, but perhaps a sick or old individual just forgets.

Above left: **A parasitised caterpillar, wasp larvae emerging from within its body**

Above: **The variety of snakes is astonishing. This is a highly venomous coral snake**

Hidden Dangers

One Christmas Day filming session brought its own surprise, and one that I managed to capture on film for a change. Two small spiny rats had been regularly visiting the fallen fruit and feasting for twenty minutes at a time. One of them had discovered a small hole in a fallen, rotting branch within my vision and filming range. When it had eaten a couple of the fruits it started taking others back to the hole – it was putting aside its next meal. A flash of movement caught my eye as its companion leapt into the air. I hadn't even spotted the snake – had it been there when I climbed into my hide? The fer-de-lance is one of the most venomous snakes in the forest. Almost invisible against the leaf litter, it is also lightning fast when it wants to be. Yet this time it had missed its target: even the most dangerous can have a tough time here.

A fer-de-lance snake – one of the most poisonous in the forest

How to Eat a Tarantula

My Canadian friend and tarantula expert, Rick West, is a world authority on tarantulas. He is also bug mad. Our friendship had begun in the Amazonian forest of Venezuela. Rick had asked me if I wanted to make a film about forest Indians who both worshipped and ate the world's largest tarantula, known to science as *Theraphosa blondi*. I was captivated by the story and it was to be the start of one of the most fascinating experiences in my life. The forest floor held many secrets that I was, as yet, unaware of.

The giant tarantula is truly a giant. Its legs can comfortably span a dinner plate, it has eight eyes and fangs up to 1 inch (2.5 cm) long. The venom glands are the largest of any known spider, but, thankfully, it is not at all aggressive – unless threatened.

"The tarantula was roasted on top of the fire and was surprisingly tasty; it reminded me of crab. Finally, the shaman picked up one of the fangs and used it as a toothpick!"

Deep in its subterranean lair, the tarantula feasts on a normally lethal fer-de-lance snake

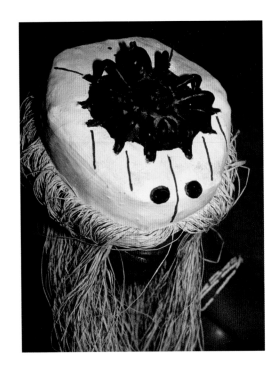

The Piaroa Indians inhabit the northern range of Amazonia in Venezuela. It is a stunningly beautiful area with spectacular mountains rising almost vertically from the forest. One of them, called Wahari Kuawai, is a sacred place to the Piaroa. Rick, our fixer-cum-guide Julio and myself had persuaded the Piaroa shaman to allow us to accompany him on a hunt for the giant tarantula. They are a few months that I don't think Rick or I will ever forget.

The rituals preceding the hunt took us all by surprise. The shaman has first to communicate with his spirits – especially that of the giant tarantula. Squatting on a log wearing a tarantula head mask, he inhales something the Piaroa call *yoppo*, a powder made up from the seeds of a forest tree. Once up there on his higher level of consciousness, he told me that he sees the spirits of family and friends, and the animals. On this occasion he was praying to the tarantula, asking it to lay more eggs and so provide his people with more food. He also told me that sometimes he sees devilish spirits trying to steal the spiders from him.

All of this was mesmerising until he insisted, or rather demanded, that we snort the powder too. It was clear that if we refused our presence would no longer be permitted. I gathered that it was a simple case, as far as the shaman was concerned, of our showing respect for his culture. We realised, having watched him for half an hour, that *yoppo* was hallucinogenic. I went first and, despite the shaman being as high as a kite, he quickly realised that I was only pretending to sniff the *yoppo* from his small wooden plate.

Above left: **Ceremonial tarantula headwear.** Above right: **The shaman snorts *yoppo* so that he can see the animal spirits**

The wooden tube he held under my nose was covered in his nasal mucous and I felt my throat sealing up. I closed my eyes and snorted. There was no escape this time: he shook the dish of powder directly under the tube. My sinuses exploded and it felt as though a pneumatic drill was pounding my brain. Minutes later, having staggered outside to retch violently, I felt most odd. The next thing I knew, my assistant Gordon was shaking me out of some dream-like state. He told me I had been talking animatedly with the rock I was sitting on. None of us wanted to have to go through that again and hoped that 'showing respect' once was enough for the shaman.

Above: **Snorting *yoppo* – the ghastly price of 'respect'!**

The giant tarantula, front legs and fangs raised in defence posture

"I saw her front feet first,

padding the ground delicately in front of her.
She was enormous
and clearly 'hunting' this intruder."

Before dawn the next morning we were trudging through the forest with the shaman and two Piaroa hunters. I was amazed that he could even walk after a night on *yoppo*. Even at this hour the humidity was heavy and, lugging our heavy camera equipment, our clothes were drenched with sweat within minutes. As daylight began to filter through the trees, one of the men stopped to look at something on the ground. It was a small hole with a patch of silk-like thread in front of it.

Giant tarantulas live in burrows. They sometimes excavate their own lairs by using their feet as digging tools. They mix the soil with their silk, binding the loose earth, which they can then roll out as small lumps. Their tunnels are usually 3–6 feet (1–2 metres) in length. They sometimes take over existing underground chambers vacated by other animals such as small rodents.

Wariena, the hunter who had found the hole, snapped off a nearby piece of vine and crouched at the entrance to the burrow. He pushed the vine into the hole and began to twiddle it gently between his fingers. He said something quietly to the shaman and, very slowly, started to pull the vine out.

I saw her front feet first, padding the ground delicately in front of her. She was enormous and clearly 'hunting' this intruder. Wariena lifted his right hand, keeping the vine moving in his left. He moved his arm over her, and lowered his hand to just above the tarantula's thorax. In one quick movement, he pinned her to the ground with his thumb. He folded her eight legs back behind her abdomen and, in less than a minute, expertly wrapped her up in a large leaf. She was unharmed, but trussed and helpless. Over the next few hours they collected another seven.

The hunter holds the dead giant tarantula for me to photograph; it's ready for cooking

We came to a massive formation of rocks and were immediately cloaked in hundreds of flies and sweat bees. They didn't bite or sting us, but were infuriatingly uncomfortable. With almost every breath that we took, we inhaled them into our mouths and noses while others invaded our ears. Despite the discomfort, it was an atmospheric place and, where the rocks met the ground, there were caves. I noticed ancient paintings on the surface of one immense slab.

The Piaroa gathered wood to make a fire while we investigated the shallow caves. It soon became apparent why there were so many flies here. Peering into the first dark fissure we could see a bundle wrapped in vine leaves and lianas. It was a decomposing human body: these were the Piaroa funeral caves.

The Piaroa made a fire by rubbing two pieces of wood together. In a few minutes Wariena's companion had a small flame. The tarantulas were unwrapped and killed by pushing a small wooden spike through their bodies. The two fangs were removed and kept to one side. The large abdomen was twisted off and the contents squeezed onto a leaf. Each female produces about 70–80 eggs. The leaf was wrapped, parcel fashion, and cooked in the hot ashes at the edge of the fire for a few minutes.

I was starving, but the result was a very bitter omelette that I just couldn't stomach. The rest of the tarantula was roasted on top of the fire and was surprisingly tasty; it reminded me of crab. Finally, the shaman picked up one of the fangs and used it as a toothpick!

The shaman squats by the Piaroa funeral caves

A golden white tassel-eared marmoset bites the sharp pincers off a giant grub

Marmoset delicacies

It was during my time with the Piaroa that Rick taught me where to look and what to expect to find on the forest floor. It really was an astonishingly interesting place. During our early bug hunts I discovered exactly where to find scorpions, beetles, ants nests, frogs of every kind, snakes, lizards, spiders and, one of my favourites, venomous centipedes.

Rotting tree trunks were a constant source of exciting discoveries. Once a tree has died, numerous creatures use the decaying soft outer wood to make their homes, deposit their larvae or to find food over the many years it can take it to decompose. One afternoon while following a group of golden white tassel-eared marmosets I watched them investigate just such a decaying tree.

It was a dead Tachigalia, and the main trunk of the tree, some 100 feet (30 metres) high, had broken off about 25 feet (8 metres) above the ground. It had clearly been rotting for several years but the bark on the section of trunk still standing was very soft and numerous holes had been bored into it. The marmosets started to pull away small pieces of the flaking bark and peer into the holes. One tugged for half a minute before pulling out a huge white grub with nasty-looking jaws on its head. The larvae use them to dig their way into the tree. The tiny monkey leapt to a sapling close by and, with one audible crunch, mashed the jaws and head disarming the grub. It then fed on it with gusto.

The rest of the group started making loud alarm calls and scattered around the 10-foot (3-metre) circumference of the dead trunk. They were all staring at the same place, a large piece of dislodged bark just 3 feet (1 metre) above the ground. There, bristling its many legs, was the largest venomous centipede I had ever seen. I remembered Rick telling me they were the one critter that really 'creeped him out'!

Scolopendra gigantea is a predatory arthropod (an invertebrate with a segmented body, jointed limbs, and external skeleton) that feeds on lizards, frogs and even small birds. This one was about 10 inches (25 centimetres) long with an elongated flattened body of 21 segments, most of which bore a pair of legs. It can move with astonishing speed and clearly, handling it would be most unwise.

The marmosets' behaviour certainly told me that they knew what the *Scolopendra*'s armoury could inflict. They moved about it with purpose, leaping away as it reared its flaying body towards the closest attacker. It took a minute for them to get the better of it. Eventually, as one marmoset attacked the tail, the centipede reared its head and upper body and another marmoset, with precision timing, grabbed it just under the head and bit it repeatedly. After the male who had killed it had eaten for a minute, the others chased him for their share. Ten minutes later, as I watched through my binoculars, an adult male held what remained at arms' length for two infants to feed on it.

Frolicking Frogs

Frogs have been Mike Linley's lifelong passion. He's world renowned as a herpetologist and was *Survival's* scientific advisor. He's also a friend and expert bug hunter. It was Mike who introduced me to the leaf-litter variety of toad. When I first took him into the forest surrounding my camp, we hadn't been walking five minutes when he became animated. Peering closely at the leaf litter, he pointed to a dying leaf – at least that's what it looked like to me. Then he picked it up and showed me the most perfectly camouflaged toad I had ever seen. Perfectly patterned to resemble a leaf, coloured in mottled browns, blacks and golds –

even the vein that runs down the centre of the leaf was there. I had been walking here for several years and had never seen them.

At that time, the height of the dry season, river levels were falling rapidly. One evening at about ten o'clock I was fast asleep in my hammock when something woke me. Outside, and very close to my hut, a tremendous din of loud croaks had struck up. Even I knew they were frogs – but what kind? I could see Mike getting dressed by torchlight and when I asked him what was happening, he replied in excited hushed tones, '*Phyllomedusa bicolor* – and they're mating!'

Tiny leaf toads mimic the patterns of leaves to camouflage themselves from prey and predators on the forest floor

Outside, we turned our torches off. My hut sits in a small forest clearing and a near full moon cast enough light for us to follow the trail to the creek. Fast-flowing, shallow water shimmered just 100 feet (30 metres) in front of us. Trees towered above, marking the edge of the forest, where darkness would return; their massive crowns silhouetted against the sky seemed to be watching us.

A small enclosure with a pool of still water, which we had built to house a rescued terrapin, was the setting for tonight's show. A branch drooped from the tree overhead, its leafy tip just an arm's length above the surface. Our approach had silenced them and Mike switched his torch on, scanning the branch.

Eight huge, bright green, tree frogs stared at us, their big bulging eyes reflecting the light beam. Two of them were in an embrace, the male with his large padded toes wrapped tightly around the smaller female. Immediately beneath them two leaves had been fixed together forming a conical-shaped cup, and this was half full of their spawn. Mike explained that in less than a week the tadpoles would emerge; gravity would take them to the water below where only one or two would grow into adults. The others would end up as fish suppers.

Watching them courting on the branch was fascinating. Their slow movements appearing exaggerated, bringing a cinematic slow-motion effect to the scene. I wondered why this noisy get-together didn't attract a predator and assumed that they must be unpalatable. It wasn't until six months later, when we met the Matis Indians, that I discovered why the giant monkey frog, as it was called, would never be dish of the day on any creature's menu (see page23).

"Eight **huge,** bright green, tree frogs **stared at us,** their **big** bulging eyes reflecting the light beam. Two of them were in an embrace, the male with his **large padded toes** **wrapped tightly** around the smaller female."

Opposite: **A tree frog, its colouration remarkably similar to that of the leaf on which it is sitting.** Above: **Hylid tree frog**

On the March

At breakfast the following morning our home, my rainforest hut, was invaded by a voracious army. It happened maybe two times each year and, even though we could not have stopped them had we wanted to, they were in fact most welcome. Our house was about to get a spring clean; army ants were on the march.

Their systematic searching of every square centimetre of ground makes them one of the most effective hunters. While cockroaches and other bugs scurried from the crevices and cracks of my hut, straight into their jaws, we followed the marching columns into the forest 160 feet (50 metres) away. Each night army ants swarm together, creating what's known as a bivouac. Millions of them cling together to form a living, pulsating temporary nest. For three consecutive days they spread out at dawn, in a different direction, covering every bit of ground for 1,000 feet (300 metres) or more. On the fourth day they move house.

I spent one week following them, filming, as they caught scorpions, snakes and even cleared wasps' nests of their larvae. Nothing was safe from them, although I had the perfect solution to keep them at bay for a while. Wearing Wellington boots thickly smeared with Vaseline, I could stand in their midst and film for half an hour in relative comfort.

Camponotus ants cut open fruits to harvest the seeds within. They discard the seeds in their own 'garden' to ultimately provide more food

Working together

But army ants were only one of their kind. Scientists estimate that in parts of Amazonia ants make up four times the biomass of all land vertebrates combined. The ants, for me, were a perfect example of how puzzling this rainforest could be. They may be easy enough to find, but to understand how they fit into the bigger picture here means observing them very closely for considerable periods. Sometimes what you see can astound.

For some time I had been intrigued by clumps of strange-looking vegetation in the low *Mollia* trees overhanging a creek close to our base camp. Through binoculars it appeared as though they were football-sized mounds of earth with many plants sprouting from their surfaces. I had also noticed that our resident sloths and monkeys studiously avoided visiting these trees. I decided to build a scaffold filming tower into the crown of one, to take a closer look.

At just over 30 feet (10 metres) the height was not a problem, but the moment our metalwork touched any part of the tree our platform swarmed with rather angry *Camponotus* ants. Some quick tree pruning had to be done to liberate our position. This closer vantage point solved the first mystery: the mounds that we could see were ant's nests. They create the fabric of their home from chewed fibres and soil. As I gently touched the paper-thin surface it crumbled, then dozens of ants quickly appeared to repair the damage.

The most striking thing about their nest was the overall effect of a well-tended garden. Between the many different plants growing from the nest's outer surface, the place had been kept meticulously clean, weeded of unwanted growth.

One species that sprouted in several places bore mature shiny purple fruits. With my camera just a couple of inches (5 centimetres) from one I watched as several ants worked their jaws back and forth through the fruits' outer covering. These tiny ants had to work hard to open a small hole in the grape-sized fruit, but once they were through I could see what they were after – seeds.

Each minute seed had a thin, translucent layer around it. Over the next hour, one by one, the ants struggled to pull them free, then carried each seed back to the nest, disappearing inside along thin branches that were incorporated into the main structure. Away from our prying camera the ants would eat the thin fleshy layer around the seed, which they then discarded. This seed, perfectly placed in the nutrient-rich matter of their nest, would germinate and take root. Months from now the same plant would bear fruit and the whole process would start again. This was indeed an ant garden, but there was much more of this story to uncover than we could have believed.

Above right: **Seeds abandoned by the ants sprout from the ant garden, which provides camouflage and food**

The *Mollia* tree was itself bearing many fruits. Although they were some two to three months away from maturity, groups of tiny insects clustered under the base of each young fruit gave a clue as to why the ants want to live here. They are aphids, tiny, soft-bodied almost pear-shaped insects. Related to the cicadas, they have relatively long legs and antennae, but what makes them special to the *Camponotus* ants are two small tubes called cornicles that protrude from their back end.

The aphids' mouths are designed to suck fluid from plants, and this brings them into conflict with many modern gardeners. But in this *Mollia* tree they only ever feed from the exact spot where the fruit is attached to its stem. Biologists believe that they have poor digestive systems and therefore excrete, for their size, large quantities of a sweet liquid called 'honeydew' from their cornicles. It is this bounty that attracts the ants and to get it they must tend the aphids as though they were prize herds. Their industry is a marvel to watch through a macro lens. Often, if I had

finished early for the day, I would pass hours on that platform following the ants' busy antics just for the pure pleasure of it.

The ants are the reason no other animals attempt to feed on *Mollia* foliage or fruits. The aphids have exclusive access to the tree's lifeblood, they are protected by the ants' presence and the ants never have to leave the mollia tree. It's a perfectly self-contained community. But if monkeys and others cannot use the tree, how does it ensure its seeds are dispersed?

It's always found near creeks and small rivers. The tree times the maturity of its fruits to coincide with high water season in April and May. At this time the pods dry out in the sun, burst open and cast their seeds. They fall on to water. Like millions of other trees, countless animals and many of the native humans here, the *Mollia* has had to adapt to one of the natural world's most amazing phenomena. For up to six months, 62,000 square miles (almost 100,000 square kilometres) of the Amazon rainforest is under water.

The componotus ants herd the bugs for the honeydew that they excrete

CHAPTER 6

Water World – The Flooded Forest

"The water was still and clear as glass: the trunks of the trees stood up from it, their branches dipped into it... the reflection of every leaf was so perfect that wood and water seemed to melt into each other, and it was difficult to say where one began and the other ended. Silence and shade so profound brooded over the whole scene that the mere ripple of our paddles seemed a disturbance."

Professor and Mrs Louise Agassiz
A Journey in Brazil (1868)

I am standing on the forest floor between the trunks of two 130-feet (40-metre) tall trees. The aerial roots of an air plant drop vertically from a high branch and where they touch the forest floor I recognise a dark hole, the entrance to an armadillo den that I filmed last year. It's almost midday and shafts of brilliant sunshine spotlight patches of the silt-covered carpet of fallen leaves. My brain is trying to reconcile the images; they are verging on the surreal. The difficulty of walking normally enhances the feeling of being trapped in a dream and, letting go of the camera, my eyes follow it as it floats towards the treetops. This is a place I know well – but where I walked just a few weeks ago, I now swim. My depth gauge tells me that I'm at just over 30 feet (10 metres).

Every year during the wet season, January through June, more than 6½ feet (2 metres) of rain drenches Amazonia. The rivers, more than one thousand of them, overflow and inundate vast areas of the rainforest. The deluge does not kill the trees, quite the opposite. This dynamic ecosystem has adapted to thrive in these unique conditions because the seasonal flood brings huge amounts of sediment, rich nutrients that feed the flora and fauna of this underwater forest.

The torrential rains create an aquatic environment where some of the most unexpected and rare wildlife flourish. Every year fish, aquatic animals and reptiles migrate, some in enormous numbers, to these new fertile habitats to reproduce before returning to the main rivers as the floodwater recedes. To journey into it is to discover a water world of staggering beauty and diversity.

Opposite: Filming in the flooded forest, I was never quite sure what lurked beneath the surface of the water

River Wolves

My first experience of this half-drowned forest happened in the interior of Guyana in 1987. I was there to make my first television special about giant otters. At that time my home was on the Hebridean Island of Mull, where I had spent many hours following and photographing our shy and secretive native otters. I could never have imagined that I would soon be filming their South American relatives, and that they were bigger than me, snacked on piranha and lived in groups of a dozen or more. My first face-to-face encounter with them took my breath away.

Black, mirror-like water undulated as the two canoes moved forward. My guides, local Macusi men, had that innate ability to dip a paddle into water and propel the dugout without making a sound. We moved smoothly between the tree trunks, their crowns just a few metres above our heads. A brilliant shimmering green hummingbird flew in front of my face and hovered just an arm's length away. The hum of its wings beating at 25 times a second mesmerised me. A rasping snort shocked me into awareness and the bee-sized flying jewel was gone in a flash. I was left wondering whether it had really happened, but what on earth was that?

The giant otter, the largest otter in the world. Once killed for its fur to make handbags it was taken to the brink of extinction

A giant otter feasts on a large black piranha fish. The otter's eyes are especially adapted to enable it to hunt under water

A young Caboclo boy fishing with a harpoon. Fish migrate into the flooded forest each year to breed

I would certainly have been anxious had my companions not been smiling. Four, five, then six large brown heads bobbed up and down in the water ahead of us. Snorts and loud coughs sent sprays of mist into the air. I could see cream-coloured throat bibs and their formidable teeth. Like periscopes, their muscular bodies rose through the surface then fell back, to give them a better view of us. They were so utterly huge that it took a while to accept that they really were otters. Their curiosity only lasted three or four minutes, but their vocalisations continued, echoing off trees and water, for much longer. They had moved away through the trees to our right and we decided to follow them.

Like some Disneyesque scene, morpho butterflies the size of plates danced around us on this water ride, their impossibly iridescent blue wings catching sunlight that dazzled me. Several large iguanas stared out from branches that should have been 65 feet (20 metres) or more above us, but we were moving among them. Occasionally one would leap into the water and disappear without a trace. But this wasn't fantasy; it was far too beautiful to have been man made. Then, my reverie was shattered once more by unearthly wails and screams.

Our canoes emerged from the trees into full sunlight. The gap was only about 160 feet (50 metres) wide, a clearly defined river for half the year, but for now dry land only existed as a narrow muddy bank 10 feet (3 metres) above the water on the far side. There, several trees had fallen into the water creating a tangled mass of boughs and branches, where twelve giant otters were making a din of almost ear-splitting proportions. One of

the males had caught a very large tiger fish, I guessed at least 15 pounds (7 kg) in weight, and he was trying to protect his catch from the greedy intentions of his family.

Using the support of a partly submerged tree trunk he violently thrashed his long powerful tail, sending plumes of water into the air. He managed to hang on to the hefty catfish with his teeth, all the while growling loudly at the others. They swam about him in a highly excited state, screaming in a manner that had to be heard to be believed. I could see why the locals called these impressive creatures River Wolves.

"They almost **bumped into the black caiman,** which whipped its **considerable tail** around. Despite the impressive **show of teeth and its size,** it was clearly the one having to defend itself. All five **otters** mobbed it from both sides. The caiman could easily have killed one otter, but as a group they were **invincible.**"

Growing to over 6.5 feet (2 metres) in length and weighing more than 66 pounds (30 kg), they are the largest otter in the world. Their heads are rounded with tiny ears set to the sides, although they have extremely acute hearing. A blunt nose and two eyes adapted for seeing under water give them a rather bug-eyed appearance. Short, thick, strong legs have large webbed feet that propel them at great speed under water and sharp claws that secure struggling prey. They catch and consume on average about 9 pounds (4 kilograms) of fish every day. Males tend to be a little larger than the females, but what sets them all apart from each other are the cream-coloured blotches on their throats. Every pattern is unique and this is how I became proficient at recognising individuals from the different groups that I followed.

Twelve was the largest family I ever found; most of the others I saw varied between four and nine otters. Interestingly, in all my years in those regions, I never came across a solitary giant otter. They evidently lived in highly organised social units and some zoologists believe they occasionally coordinate searching for prey as a pack, similar to wolves or wild dogs. Sadly, despite their superb hunting ability, they were almost wiped out last century for their pelts. Luxurious, dense brown, velvety giant otter fur was much sought after by the fashion industry and their noisy, territorial and social disposition made them easy targets. Fortunately though, like the jaguar, they were to escape extinction because of legislation prohibiting trade in their skins.

A black caiman, one of the most deadly predators of Amazonia

One year later, on the same Guyanese riverside, I was filming two small giant otter cubs emerging from their birth holt for the first time. Otters excavate their own compartmental system of chambers in the riverbanks where the group sleeps in smaller family units but all very close together. They give birth to between one and four cubs after a pregnancy lasting 65 to 70 days. The young are delightfully clumsy when they first appear, their heads and feet looking disproportionately big. All members of the family care for the infants.

Adult giant otters fiercely defend their young and will attack an adversary as a group. I observed this behaviour late one afternoon when the family I was following were moving up stream towards the den where they would spend the night.

Three adults, with two one-year-old juveniles, were swimming mid river, their heads surfacing alternately as they came up to breathe. The remaining two otters were galumphing along the muddy river edge, occasionally splashing into the water. They almost bumped into the 10-foot (3-metre) caiman, but their approach had been noticed. The caiman whipped its considerable tail around, snarling a warning to keep away. Despite the impressive show of teeth and its size, the black caiman was clearly the one having to defend itself in this amazing confrontation.

All five adults mobbed it from both sides at the same time. The caiman could easily have killed one otter, but as a group they were invincible. Meanwhile the young otters stayed out of the affray a few metres away in a tangle of fallen branches. The caiman waited its chance and escaped by launching itself into the water, finding sanctuary in the muddy depths.

An underwater view of the flooded forest

Fruit-eating Fish

During two years of following giant otters, I learnt much about the igapo, as this type of flooded forest is called. Four years after my giant otter film was completed, I was living in Alligator Creek, my long-term home camp in Brazil's Amazonas State. For half the year it, too, was isolated by igapo. Here I met two dedicated student icthyologists, working on the migratory movements of fish. I quickly became infected by their passion for the subject.

To be realistic, accurate estimates of fish species that live here simply cannot be made because there are still unknown numbers remaining to be discovered. However, there are over 2,000 known species to date and some experts estimate more that 3,000 is nearer to the truth. One fact that is not challenged is that these fish depend on the rainforest for their very survival.

Many of the flooded forest fish have evolved to eat fallen fruits. The trees have come to rely on many of those fish to disperse their seeds. Indeed, some seeds will not germinate unless they have passed through the gut of a fish. The most famous fish in Amazonas, and certainly my favourite on the forest barbecue, is tambaqui, *Colossoma macropomum*.

This colossus can reach 3 feet (1 metre) in length and weigh more than 60 pounds (30 kilograms). The adults have broad molar teeth that are specialised for crushing fruit and seeds. The tambaqui is well known in Amazonia for gathering underneath rubber trees when the fruits are mature. The pods burst, scattering the seeds into the water, and they are one of the tambaqui's favourite foods. As the floodwaters begin to recede, the tambaqui's massive body is a storehouse of fat, gleaned from feasting on seeds for several months, which it uses to survive through the lean times of the dry season.

Vegetarian fish – tambaqui. Their huge bodies are fuelled by the fat from the seeds that they eat

As the rains fall, the rivers swell and flood much of the forest

Giants of the Deep

The fruit-eating tambaqui is big, but it is nowhere near the biggest fish here. Many Amazonian catfish grow to seriously impressive sizes. The largest scaled freshwater fish in the world, known locally as the pirurucu (*Arapaima gigas*) can grow, if left alone, to over 8 feet (2.5 metres) and weigh over 220 pounds (100 kilograms). Nowadays, because of overfishing, they average 6.5 feet (2 metres) long and only 150 pounds (70 kilograms). Pirurucu are superb predators that lie in weight on the riverbed and wait for their meal to deliver itself. If a fish swims close by, their jaws open so quickly that the prey is sucked, helpless, into the cavernous mouth.

This astonishing place surprises one at every turn, even in the fish world. There are vegetarian piranha, the cara folha, a fish that looks more like a leaf than a leaf, and the water monkey (*Osteoglossum ferreirai*), known locally as Aruana, which leaps from the water and grabs insect prey from overhanging branches. The adult male also accompanies its young and, when it senses danger, rapidly opens his huge mouth sucking them all in. The infants are only released when the threat has passed.

And then there is the peixe-boi, or ox-fish (*Trichechus inunguis*) – only it isn't a fish at all, it's a manatee, and a very rare one today.

It was as though a submarine had committed itself to surfacing but at the last minute decided instead to dive at full speed. Justinho, a local fisherman, and I were paddling slowly across a shallow lake when the surface erupted just a few metres in front of us. There was a tremendous commotion and Justinho laughed, bellowing, 'peixe-boi', Portuguese for the Amazonian manatee. Our tiny canoe lurched heavily as the waves hit us.

Manatees are massive aquatic mammals. Completely vegetarian, these gentle giants have been hunted to the point of extinction and to see one today is a rare privilege. They belong to the taxonomic order of Sirenia, named after the infamous Greek sirens that lured sailors to their deaths. The peixe-boi could never be described as beautiful, but it does have a soft, gentle, endearing nature that is quite captivating. It is the only truly freshwater manatee in the world, and it is restricted uniquely to Amazonia.

Their enormous dark grey bodies grow to an average length of 9 feet (2.75 metres) and can weigh over 1,000 pounds (480 kilograms). Smooth skinned, small eyed, they have a gigantic paddle-like tail that can give them an astonishing burst of speed. They have two fore-flippers which, if x-rayed, show the ancient bone

"Manatees are **massive** aquatic mammals. Completely vegetarian, these gentle giants have been **hunted to the point of extinction** and to see one today is a rare privilege. They're named after the infamous Greek sirens **that lured sailors** to their deaths!"

An Amazonian manatee feeding on aquatic vegetation

structure of hands. In 1992 I filmed manatees under water, using these 'hands' to pull aquatic vegetation into their mouths while they were feeding.

Like all manatees, the peixe-boi has a very low metabolic rate that enables it to hold its breath for long periods, sometimes useful when trying to avoid human predators. When it does surface to breathe it does so silently, through two large valved nostrils that remain shut under water. The peixe-boi migrate in synchronisation with the seasonal floods and feed exclusively on aquatic grasses and plants. Their molar teeth can munch through almost 90 pounds (40 kilograms) of this vegetation a day, their digestive system perfectly adapted to process the high-fibre, low-protein diet. The food may take up to a week to pass through the digestive system, during which time they produce a great deal of methane gas. Amazonian manatees unquestionably suffer from flatulence.

It was, and still is, man's ignorant pursuit of this mammal combined with the creature's very slow reproduction rate that has brought *Trichechus inunguis* to the brink of extinction. Sexual maturity is reached sometime between five and ten years of age, and even then they only produce one calf every three to five years. And this highlights the fact that, due to their rarity and understandably shy nature, very little is known about Amazonian manatees in the wild. Excellent research work in captivity and with field studies has been continuing for some years through the National Amazonian Research Institute (INPA), in Manaus, but their scientists battle against immense odds.

A female Amazonian manatee and a juvenile. The manatee has been mercilessly hunted for decades

The House of Them

Apart from humans, the only other potential predator on manatees, at least on young peixe-boi calfs, is Amazonia's largest reptile, the black caiman (*Melanosuchus niger*). In the igapo it was usually only their heads that I saw, as they moved away from our presence. In a similarly depressing tale to that of the manatee, black caiman too have been slaughtered in their thousands over the decades. Today they are certainly faring better than the peixe-boi, but to film them I would have to wait until the flooded forest had largely dried out, for this is when they congregate to breed.

'No Sir, don't go there, it's the House of Them'. Despite the scorching 100°F (39°C) heat, small shivers of cold fear coursed through me as he spoke. These were the first words of an irresistible horror story that pulled me into a situation that could have cost the lives of three people, including my own.

Argentino looked much older than his forty-five years. Squatting on the steps of his hut, he wore a permanent look of deep worry on his face. I couldn't help but stare at what remained of his right arm, a scarred stump severed halfway between where his elbow used to be and his

shoulder. He has lived on the banks of the Madeira River in Brazil all of his life, his home a ramshackle hut just a few hours' paddle away from Lake Acara. There was no way on this earth that he was going to take me to Acara, the place he called the House of Them. He never wanted to see the lake again. But somehow I had to get there.

Lake Acara used to be a place where the few people who lived in the region could fill their nets with fish within minutes of casting them. It's a very different story today. Argentino is living proof that to go fishing there now is to risk life and limb. In the nearest communities everyone can tell you the name of someone who has been killed or seriously injured there.

After the rain season floodwaters have receded, Acara is cut off from the main river by miles of dense forest. Two creeks feed the lake, but for most of the year they are impossible to navigate due to fallen trees. For my film crew and me there was only one way in. We would have to slog 5 miles (8 kilometres) through rainforest, cross a fly-infested swamp and then paddle across the lake's deceptively benign surface – and, of course, get back. I never considered for one moment that we wouldn't make it.

Like all alligators, the dwarf caiman regulates its body temperature throughout the day by leaving the water; the sun heats the animal up while the water cools it down

Acara is the breeding ground of one of Amazonia's most endangered and feared predators, the black caiman. They breed in the forest surrounding the lake and I desperately wanted to film them in the wild. After a decade in this rainforest it was one of the few animals I had yet to get really close to. At first we were able to persuade a local fisherman to take us to the mouth of one of the feeder creeks. When we arrived there, three hours up stream from the main river, a black cloud swirled above us – vultures. The air was rancid and the stench of death made us all gag.

With cloths covering our mouths and noses we left our canoes and went into the edge of the forest to discover what I already suspected. I counted more than 25 huge black caiman heads, each with bullet holes in the top of the skull. The rotting remains of their bodies lay everywhere as the vultures squabbled all about us. It was a sad and shocking scene and we all stared at it in silence. This was no attempt to cull the black caiman for safety reasons. Two large canoes lay near by, their cargo abandoned because of our approach. I lifted the tarpaulins and looked down at white flesh, masses of it. Our guide, Dandi, was visibly very nervous and insisted we leave. The perpetrators were armed and no doubt hiding, watching us from the darkness of the forest. We filmed the scene in the forlorn hope that a copy given to the authorities might have some effect.

On our way back to the main river I worried about the lake. If the hunters had somehow continued along that creek and entered Acara, what carnage could they have created there? But the creek was impassable I had been told and, with this thought, we set off at dawn the next day by foot to find the House of Them.

We emerged from the forest edge at five-thirty, the light of day coming fast. It was heavy going through swamp grass for the first hour but we settled into a rhythm and just absorbed the stunning scenery surrounding us at sunrise. Two local fishermen, Bentino and Vanderclay, were leading us in. Behind them were cameraman Brian Sewell, my co-producer Andie Clare, then me. Following some distance behind us were Valquimar, my fixer, and another local hunter, Francisco.

I only just caught a glimpse of it as came from under Andie's feet and whipped over, hitting the toecap of my left boot. I instinctively jumped and yelled and saw the 2 foot (60 cm) long dark shape slither fast into the waist-deep grass. My heart was pounding as I realised just how close I had come to being bitten by what Francisco had called 'Surucucu'. We knew it as Lachesis muta, the scientific name that translated, means 'silent fate' in English, the bushmaster. Andie was amazed that she had trodden on it without coming to grief! In true Colonel Fawcett style, I announced to my companions that due to the necrotic qualities of the snake's venom, my boot toecap was dying an agonisingly slow death, dissolving from the inside out!

Over 25 huge black caiman heads with bullet holes in the top of the skull lay rotting on the forest floor

"...in front of us, it looked as though someone had **laid stepping-stones across the lake.**
Hundreds of them! They were black caiman
and I stared **wide-eyed, thrilled,** at the revelation
but realising we had somehow to get through them...
I knew I was
really scared because for the first time in my life
I couldn't have given a damn about my camera equipment."

The lake was huge, perhaps 12 square miles (20 square kilometres), and the distant forest edge, our destination, almost invisible. Biting flies plagued us as we sank up to our thighs in mud. Then we found the canoes. Hewn from trees, they were small and shallow, meant for one person but just big enough for two. The lake perimeter was mud with a few centimetres of water covering it, so we had to push the canoes in the hope that deeper water would materialise. The temperature was rising quickly and before eight o'clock we were exhausted. Then the water deepened slightly, enough to push the paddles into the mud below to give our canoes propulsion. Then I saw them.

Half a kilometre in front of us, it looked as though someone had laid stepping-stones across the lake. Hundreds of them! They were black caiman and I stared wide-eyed, thrilled, at the revelation but realising we had somehow to get through them in order to reach the forest. All around us thousands of fish flapped on the surface, dying in the shallow fetid water while the caiman snapped and swallowed them.

Bentino, paddling with great care, explained that the caiman we could see were not the problem.

Underneath us there was about 7 feet (2 metres) of soft mud and this was where many of the big caiman kept cool. This is where Argentino's paddle had disturbed a 'grande' and it had tipped his canoe over. Seconds later his right arm had been ripped off.

It was a nightmarish scene and I stared at the mirror-like surface. There, just a few centimetres of water lay between terror and me. I knew I was really scared because for the first time in my life I couldn't have given a damn about my camera equipment – it was insured! Without warning a commotion erupted beneath my canoe and a caiman tail surfaced, thrashing water into the boat. Rigid with fear, I baled as fast as I could. The tiny boat rocked but didn't tip over. My hands were shaking as I shouted to the other canoes behind me that we should back off.

I had miscalculated the logistics of our journey. The muddy lake water was hot and undrinkable and it was now obvious that we could not return by the same route, it was just too shallow. Eventually we had to abandon the canoes and wade through the waist deep mud without shelter from the fierce heat for almost two hours. By one o'clock three of us were close to collapse through dehydration. I have no

doubt that it was only the forethought of Vanderclay's father, who trekked in from our base camp with supplies of fresh bottled water, that saved our lives that day.

I was in a state of collapse and the following day I was taken by boat to a community that boasted what could loosely be called a hospital. I spent two days on painkillers and a re-hydration drip. Despite our ordeal, we all recovered and returned to the lake just two weeks later. Some rain had fallen and the water level had risen a little, making our passage easier. This time I did find the caimans' nesting ground in the forest behind the lake and filmed it.

Four weeks after our second expedition Argentino's brother and a friend went to the lake to fish. In the early morning while laying their nets they disturbed a black caiman. Their canoe overturned and they were attacked. Argentino's brother's companion was killed; he was the first to be savagely bitten. His brother survived but, in a final twist that seems stranger than fiction, he lost his left arm.

We had somehow survived Acara – but The House of Them had claimed two more victims.

Dotted with partially submerged black caiman, the surface of Lake Acara was a spectacular, yet frightening, sight as we paddled our canoe across it

Tucuxi river dolphins on the Rio Branco. They are related to the marine species and are much smaller than the pink Amazon river dolphin, or boto

The Big Pink

In a land that overflows with water and extraordinary forms of plants and animals, it is perhaps fitting that one of the most visually arresting sights is a pink dolphin swimming between the upper branches of forest trees.

The Amazon River dolphin, also known as the boto or big pink, *Inia geoffrensis*, is uniquely adapted to the Amazon River system and flooded forest. It's the largest of all river dolphins, reaching a length of almost 10 feet (3 metres) and almost 220 pounds (100 kilograms) in weight. The dolphins' distribution throughout the Amazon is significantly affected by the annual migration of fish into the flooded forest.

Botos have small eyes but highly developed echolocation senses. They have supremely flexible bodies and, because of special vertebrae that aren't fused together as in other dolphins, can sweep their heads from side to side to grab prey. This is a useful adaptation in the underwater forest among jumbled trees and branches. Their mouths are beak like, containing over one hundred teeth that are deceptively lethal, and botos are known to feed on more than fifty species of fish.

If I ever needed proof of their intelligence, which I didn't, one afternoon while our 70-ton riverboat was moored to the edge of a sandbank on the upper Rio Branco, two boto dolphins put on a terrific display of co-operative hunting skills. The steep, 6½-feet (2-metre)-high sandbank sloped sharply into deep water. It stretched away from our boat for about 300 feet (100 metres) before bending ninety degrees towards the middle of the river. At this point this created a narrow spit of sand that was just above the water.

My assistant, Gordon, and I were standing on the top deck with an elevated view of the whole scene when I noticed a boto dolphin lying on the surface, almost motionless, at right angles to the end of the sand bar. I was pointing the dolphin out to Gordon, when a large fish appeared from under our boat and raced at tremendous speed along the river surface following the contour of the sandbank. Just 3 feet (1 metre) behind it and going at a pace one would have thought impossible for its size, a boto pursued, creating an impressive bow-wave.

We were so involved in watching the chase that I had forgotten about the first dolphin. It hadn't moved, though; the trap was set. The fish, even at almost 20 miles (30 kilometres) an hour, spotted it and instinctively leapt for its life; straight out of the water and about 4 feet (1.5 metres) onto the beach.

Thinking it had escaped, we cheered as it flapped about, but our shouts were cut short with shock as the dolphin that had lain in wait launched itself onto the beach, grabbed the fish and, with twists and turns, got itself back into the river. Gordon and I stared wide-eyed and in unison shouted 'wow'!

The boto is surrounded by much legend and superstition. An elder at a Yanomami Indian community once told me that several of the young girls in his tribe had been made pregnant by the pink dolphin. According to the girls, late at night the boto leaves the river and magically changes into a handsome young Yanomami boy whose advances they simply are unable to resist. Whatever the flights of fancy taken by the human mind, it is this very kind of lore that has saved the boto from the fate so many other creatures have suffered. It is strictly taboo to kill them in most cultures in Amazonia. Even today, they are present in many areas, but they are extremely vulnerable and, of course, continue to be threatened by the evils of other human follies such as pollution.

Bird's-eye Views

The most special times in the flooded forest for me were after we had built a filming platform into the trees. Each day for weeks I would canoe from my camp through the igapo to the tree where we had built a bush ladder. The water was only about 20 feet (6 metres) deep here, and the platform just 13 feet (4 metres) above the surface. Almost every day would present some exciting encounter or sight.

For most of the time there was a deep stillness to the igapo. Apart from buzzing insects, the whir of hummingbird wings and the plopping of fruit into to the water it was surprisingly quiet most of the time.

Once I heard something large break the surface beneath me and take in a gasp of air. Thinking it was a boto, I looked over the edge of my camera platform and was stunned to see an adult tapir. It was the first wild one I had ever seen.

On several occasions from that perch in the trees, I watched three-toed sloths do something unusual. I was accustomed to seeing them upside-down in the trees, where they seemed to spend as much time as possible doing as little as possible. I even filmed them descending to the dry forest floor once a week or so, where they would dig a hole with their stumpy tail and deposit their droppings. But, until now, I had never seen them swimming and they are, despite appearances, very adept in the water.

The sloth is not in any sense aquatic, but if crossing water is the only way to move to new food sources then it will resort to swimming. The first one I ever filmed had a tiny baby on her back. I actually got into the water alongside them and filmed under water. She swam slothfully slowly, of course, but those clawed arms were surprisingly efficient.

The baby held its head erect like a miniature periscope, straining to keep its face above water; although it was completely immersed many times, with each dunking it instinctively held its breath.

An underwater view of the tapir

A rare view of a Brazilian tapir feeding on vegetation in a rainforest creek

A male three-toed sloth perfectly reflected in the black water of the flooded forest. Where the upper branches of the trees do not interconnect, the sloth must descend to the ground. When the forest is flooded, it has to swim to the next tree

After ten years, I can look back and remember many wonderful experiences in that flooded world. Moments that excited me, such as when the tapir appeared, immediately spring to mind. Or the time that I felt something tickle my bare knee while setting up a film shot on the bottom of a creek. It was only when I casually looked down, thinking it was a twig or leaf that needed brushing away, that I saw the head of a 10-foot (3-metre) anaconda, its tongue 'tasting' my knee. It's a good thing Colonel Percy wasn't with our crew or he would have shot the poor snake.

"His huge paws swept rhythmically below him and without hurry. Keeping his whiskers clear of the water he seemed to hold his head with a rather regal countenance. Eater of Souls Only subtle movements of water created by the remained a few minutes longer. That was the last I saw of him."

Without doubt, the most memorable moment came late one afternoon when I was just thinking about packing my gear away and paddling back to camp. The tree that my small platform was nailed to had a massive bromeliad growing from it just under the boards. A large red flower had appeared and I was laying face down, my head over the edge, looking down into the epiphyte. As I watched two beetles crawling into it, something else caught the edge of my vision.

The water below was clear but dark, stained with tannins from the local vegetation. Shafts of sunlight that struck the surface gave it a deep golden colour that was fittingly atmospheric. Where trees and vegetation met the water surface, reflections were so faultless that you usually couldn't make out where reality ended and mirror image began. That is unless the water was moving; and at this moment it was.

They were gentle undulations at first, but I instinctively knew something large was about

because these shallow waves were too uniform, and big, to have been caused by a fish. I didn't move a muscle; just lay there scanning the water with my eyes, excited and frustrated. Many trees, especially palms, prevented a distant or wide view. I couldn't hear anything either, like splashing water noises or breathing. I was staring at the perfect reflection of a thin jauari palm trunk when the image fractured.

The high angle of view from what now felt like a flimsily constructed platform meant I could see through the surface and about 3 feet (1 metre) under water. His huge paws swept rhythmically below him and without hurry. Keeping his whiskers clear of the water he seemed to hold his head with a rather regal countenance. His tail snaked out along the surface behind him, occasionally flicking to one side or the other. In less than thirty seconds he had disappeared from view. Only subtle movements of water created by the Eater of Souls remained a few minutes longer. That was the last I saw of him.

CHAPTER 7

Threatened Forest

The fate of Amazonia is, quite rightly, the focus of universal concern. For the past twenty years the developed world has heard much about the fragility of the rainforest and how important its preservation is in a global sense. The reality, sadly, is that wherever man intrudes on our planet the environment inevitably suffers – due, almost entirely, to money and politics.

Every part of Amazonia is endangered one way or another. The rivers are being overfished to the point where local human populations will soon face a crisis and the remaining indigenous peoples' very existence is under threat. Five hundred years ago, over six million people lived in the forest, yet today less than 200,000 remain. Pollution of land and water is omnipresent, but logging is the single biggest problem, especially unlawful extraction. The Brazilian government estimates that a staggering 80 per cent of all timber production is illegal in origin. Deforestation has been, and still is, on a scale that is difficult to understand unless you have seen it with your own eyes.

Just a few years ago I flew across the state of Rondonia to film the devastating impact of cattle ranching on the area. From Rondonia I travelled to Parà to record the wholesale destruction of that state's forest. Never-ending lines of massive trucks reminded me of army ants, as they carried their cargo of tree trunks along the highway to the timber processing plants. Flying for hours across those vast areas of cleared rainforest are depressing experiences I can never forget but one event, more than any other, remains imprinted deeply in my psyche.

One morning, in the heart of a forest remnant near Paragominas in the state of Parà, we followed a local man working with his chainsaw. In just three hours he had felled four giant emergent trees. In Portuguese I chatted to him about his life as he explained that this was the only employment available locally for someone like him. He was extremely poor and had seven children to feed. The 'boss' had given him the monstrously sized chainsaw. He was barefoot. Each tree he felled earned him about US$0.50. I wondered what he would make of a mahogany table in a foreign city's furniture store selling for £3,000 ($4,500).

The enormous tree boles were lifted onto a wagon and carried out, five at a time, to the timber concession plant less than one hour away. We accompanied them and filmed the process. There, in one building that could have housed several commercial aircraft, was the ultimate environmental nightmare. A Korean-made 128-foot (40-metre)-wide lathe rotated the massive trunks against a blade that shredded the ancient trees like toilet rolls. The wafer-thin sheets spewing from the other side were cut and glued into panels of plywood.

That same afternoon we interviewed the owner of the timber concession. Dripping in gold bracelets, a handgun holstered at his waist, he had a threatening manner and oozed indifference. He talked in a pathetically uninformed way about his sustainable logging extraction. I left Paragominas consumed with a feeling of utter hopelessness.

Opposite: The largest open-cast tin mine in the world, cleverly called Bom Futura (Good Future)

Rainforest harmony

Fruits of the forest

Human error

A Piaroa Indian settlement – natural
use of the forest

The lives of those who live here depend
upon the forest's natural resources

A vast dam restricts
the flow of water

Amazonia remains a living miracle of complexity whose potential demise is charted accurately these days by satellite imagery from space. Latest figures suggest some that some 200,000 square miles (322,000 square kilometres) have been cleared, which represents about 15 per cent of its total. According to the Brazilian government's own satellite data, at the start of the new millennium, the year 2000, deforestation was greater than at any time since 1995; even more worryingly, clearance rates are accelerating. If the destruction continues at present-day levels, scientists estimate that a 'point of no return' will occur between 2011 and 2016; within the next fifty years Amazonia may well be wiped out completely.

A miraculous change of political attitudes is needed if Amazonia is to survive in any substantial state. Existing Brazilian laws to protect indigenous lands need to be effectively enforced. This alone would protect and preserve some 20 per cent of the rainforest. However, many more solutions are required to protect Amazonia. Principally, sound economic and environmental alternatives to the present destructive practices need implementing. The lives of almost 20 million people depend upon this rainforest. Eco-tourism has enormous untapped potential that could directly benefit local communities. The forest and wildlife must pay the people who live in it so that it may itself survive. I dream that, one day, chainsaws could be replaced with binoculars and guidebooks.

The result of poor research
and planning

Spoils of the forest

Sustainability

Mahogany trees on the first leg of their journey to the outer world

Timber extraction rates are accelerating faster than ever

The seeds of man's greed

"The Brazilian government estimates that a staggering 80 per cent of all timber production is illegal in origin. Deforestation has been, and still is, on a scale that is difficult to understand."

Wild Amazon is intended to be a celebration of this unique rainforest. So what exactly is there to celebrate? Despite the understandable global doom and gloom, the fact that an enormous area of it still does exist today must give us something to cling on to. There are many good initiatives in progress and we must not give up hope for the sake of future generations. The rewards that the human race have already reaped from Amazonia in terms of timber, food, and medicines are staggering. What we risk losing is, simply, immeasurable.

Mahogany seeds

Civilisation!

Man's detritus

Man's inhumanity

Contaminating the food chain

"There are many good initiatives in progress and we **must not give up hope** for the sake of future generations. The rewards that the human race have already reaped from Amazonia in terms of timber, food, and medicines **are staggering.** What we risk losing is, simply, immeasurable."

Gold out means mercury in. The poison is absorbed by fish and those creatures who eat them – including us

Behind the Scenes

Filming and taking photographs in this spectacular rainforest is anything but easy; in fact, it is generally downright frustrating. It all comes down to light levels – the greatest photographic hurdle in Amazonia.

From an exposure point of view it is always easier to film moving images than to shoot stills pictures. We use 16mm motion picture film and, because we are using negative stock, we have a much wider exposure margin to play with than when using slide film for stills photos. To some extent, we can alter light levels back home after the images have been captured. (This is known as grading.) With stills photography, on the other hand, getting the right exposure is absolutely critical and my early expeditions usually produced what I considered to be disastrous results.

Over the years my preferences emerged through the hardest field tests imaginable for delicate camera equipment. For the first four years, I literally threw away a camera body every year and the lenses every two years. We tried waterproof boxes, then heated boxes and sackfulls of silica gel – but the fact was that at some stage we had to open the equipment boxes and at that second all surfaces became bathed in moisture. It was a battle that I fought for many years and never won.

After investing thousands of pounds/dollars in other makes of 35mm equipment, I settled on the Canon EOS system. I found it to be the most reliable and pleasurably simple to use. Most of the images in this book were taken on EOS 1s and, more recently, on EOS 1V camera bodies. I have not found any other camera that can equal them.

The metering system is accurate and easy to interpret – an important consideration in places where light conspires to frustrate a photographer more than in any other location I have worked in. Although I took light readings with the automatic metering system, I often had to compensate manually (very easily done with the EOS 1V) because of the variations in shadow and light. The most difficult situations were in dappled light, where there could be as much as six stops' difference between the extremes. If a jaguar walked into such a pool of light I would take a fast spot meter reading from its coat and then underexpose by two-thirds of a stop. It may sound complicated, but it very quickly became second nature! (At times I swear I had my own personal cloud following me about because it seemed that whenever I took a camera out of its case – wham! The sun disappeared behind a cloud before I could press the shutter.) The lenses I use most frequently are 20mm, 28–105mm, 100–400mm, 300mm 2.8 and the 180mm 3.5 macro – all Canon.

I use skylight filters to protect the front elements of all my lenses from scratches and other damage, neutral density filters under the full force of the sun, and just occasionally polarising filters to accentuate a sky or take away water reflection off wet foliage or rivers.

I also use a Hasselblad Xpan with a 45mm lens, my favourite kit for river- or forestscapes.

Due to the generally poor light levels inside the forest, many shots are taken using wide apertures – in fact mostly f/2.8 or 3.5. If I want greater depth of field I use faster film stocks; wherever possible I use a tripod because of the slowish shutter speeds. The new Canon image-stabilised lenses really help in low-light situations and can give me the equivalent of another stop of light. I find the autofocus on my camera so fast, even in those conditions, that I rarely shoot in manual mode. The one exception is when I am doing close-up work with my macro lens and then I always focus manually and often use a flashlight cabled off the camera to give the subject some shadow relief.

Whenever possible, I use Fuji slide film, especially Provia, because I prefer the way that stock represents the greens and reds in the forest. If choice is limited, however, I use any transparency film stock I can find. Seventy per cent of my shots are taken on ISO 400 film because most of my work is done in difficult lighting conditions and even that fast stock is remarkably fine grained. The remainder (mostly on the canopy towers and forest edges or rivers where there is much more light) are shot on ISO 50 or 100.

My film cameras are Arriflex SR2 high-speed super sixteen bodies with Zeiss and Canon lenses. I use Sachtler Video 18 tripod heads with carbon fibre legs. Then there are the twenty cases of ancillary equipment like the camera jib, dollys, fibre optic lights, underwater housings, infrared cameras, spotting scopes, camouflage hides and a multitude of bits and bobs to hold them all in place, or to clean and repair them. We shipped in twelve tons of scaffolding to build our canopy towers, which allowed us the privileged position that enabled many of the photographs in this book to be captured. It's no wonder we suffer from chronic bad backs!

Opposite: **Fascinated by its own reflection, a young male jaguar peers into my camera lens** (Photo by Gordon Buchanan)

Forest perch

Specialist gear

The platform that we built to film calf-birds
for David Attenborough's *Life of Birds*

We carted tons of gear about the forest. A camera jib
allowed me to film above and below water

Tree platforms

Where scaffold towers wouldn't fit, we built
platforms in the tree crowns

Bibliography

Adalardo de Oliveira, Alexandre, and Daly, Douglas C.
Florestas do Rio Negro
(Editora Schwarcz Ltda., 2001)

Attenborough, David
Private Life of Plants
(BBC Books, 1995)

Attenborough, David
The Life of Birds
(BBC Books, 1998)

Bates, Henry Water
The Naturalist on the River Amazons
(John Murray, 1864)

Benad, Gottfried and Hofmockel, Rainer
History and Perspectives of Muscle Relaxants

Fawcett, Colonel Percy Harrison
Lost Trails, Lost Cities: An Explorer's Narrative
(Funk & Wagnalls, 1953)

Gordon, Nick
Tarantulas, Marmosets and Other Stories: an Amazon Diary
(Metro, 1997)

Gordon, Nick
Tarantulas and Marmosets: an Amazon Diary
(Metro, 1998)

Gordon, Nick
Heart of the Amazon
(Metro, 2002)

Gordon, Nick
Monkeys of the Amazon
(Evans Mitchell Books, 2007)

Goulding, Michael, Smith, Nigel J. H. and Mahar, Dennis J.
Floods of Fortune: Ecology and Economy along the Amazon
(Columbia University Press, 1996)

Henderson, Andres
Palms of the Amazon
(Oxford University Press, 1995)

Mitchell, Andrew W.
The Enchanted Canopy
(Fontana/Collins, 1986)

Schomburgk, Richard
Travels in British Guiana (1922)

Schultes, Richard Evans
Where the Gods Reign: Plants and Peoples of the Columbian Amazon
(Synergetic Press, 1988)

Sick, Helmut
Birds in Brazil: A Natural History
(Princeton University Press, 1993)

Silva, Silvestre and Tassara, Helene
Fruit in Brazil
(Empresa das Artes, 1996)

Wallace, Alfred R. (Ed.), Richard Spruce
Notes of a Botanist on the Amazon and Andes
(New York; Macmillan and Company, 1908)

Acknowledgements

I have many personal debts of gratitude to individuals and organisations who have helped me over the years. In particular, I would like to thank the following for their valuable assistance and guidance and for taking the time to support me when I most needed it, which was often:

Instituto Nacional de Pesquisas da Amazonia (INPA): especially **Vera da Silva, Fernando Rosas Cesar, Bill Magnusson** and **Ronis da Silveira.**

Instituto Brasileiro do Meio Ambiente e dos Recursos Naturais Renováveis (IBAMA): Superintendant Hamilton Casara, Dr Adimir Passerinhos and **all the guards** protecting the Rio Branco nesting grounds – especially **Francisco Jordão da Silva**, for not shooting the jaguar!

Centro de Instrução de Guerra na Selva (CIGS): Colonel Barros Moura and **Gino Chaves da Rocha** for their professionalism and friendship, and the many Brazilian soldiers who supported our team.

Valquimar Souza de Araujo for fixing 'almost' every problem our crew encountered and for his entertaining, infectious enthusiasm.

Smithsonian Institute: Claude Gascon for permitting me to live in the institute's reserve and thereby film calf-birds at their lek.

The many **Piaroa, Satere Maues, Tikuna, Yanomami** and **Matis people**, whose lives I have portrayed over the years by way of images and words.

Anthony Rylands for explaining the latest taxonomy of Amazonian primates.

Rick West for tarantulas and too many other things to mention.

Nick Peake for providing me with the opportunity to witness and record the environmental cost of human stupidity in many parts of Brazilian Amazonia.

Mike Linley for a decade of supervising my Amazon productions and for checking the scientific accuracy of my words.

Nigel Blundell for being instrumental in making another book happen.

My assistants: Gordon Buchanan, for five exceptional years and the moments that he recorded on film, some of which appear in the Behind the Scenes section of this labour of love; **Stephen Terry; Ron Kiley; Almir Cavalcante**; and especially **Neil Shaw**, who filled a vital breach in our crew before the contract ink had even dried. He helped me bring my jaguar dream to its final conclusion and kept me sane in the process. They all had, to varying degrees, to put up with my obsession to capture the perfect sequence or shot.

The remarkable **Diane McTurk**, for my very first steps in Guyana's forests and for introducing me to the giant otters from which all else followed.

Rosamund Kidman-Cox, Editor of *BBC Wildlife Magazine*, for being genuinely interested in what I was doing and helping to hone my writing attempts for her marvellous publication, which I unashamedly plug.

The BBC Natural History Unit – especially **Sir David Attenborough, Peter Bassett, Jo Sarsby, Miles Barton, Mike Salisbury, Phil Hurrell** and **Di Williams.**

Antonieta Sobralino Cavalcante, for being a fantastic field assistant and organiser, for being bitten by countless creatures, for unflinching support over ten years, and therefore for having shared for much of that time the only true danger of our forest, the 'Hook of Holland and her Mad Marc'. And, of course, for accepting my proposal of marriage!

Caroline Brett and Brazil's Batman, **Wilson Ueida**, for bringing the world of vampire bats into focus for me.

Andie Clare for sharing my passion to make wildlife films in Amazonia and being brave enough to direct me at The House of Them.

Mark Gorton for helping me realise my next project, the film series *Secrets of the Amazon*.

Bill Lamar for identifying my snake images.

Alison Aitken for much support over the years and for keeping many of the Survival 'family' in touch.

Professional Colour Laboratories, Salford, Manchester, England: Bernard Wilson-Jones and his team for giving such tender care to my thousands of rolls of slide film for the past twelve years. It is always a pleasure to visit PCL, who understand my paranoia as the chemicals reveal the rainforest's secrets. Their E6 lads are simply great.

Harry Ricketts of Evans Mitchell Books (previously of Fountain Press) for everything, but especially for making the production of this book such a pleasure.

Finally, my **Editor, Sarah Hoggett**, who helped make my words make sense, and **Kip Halsey** – long time friend and confidant.

Index

Page numbers in italics refer to photographs